Kaplan Publishing are constantly finding n
difference to your studies and our exciting
offer something different to students look

This book comes with free MyKaplan onli
study anytime, anywhere. **This free onlin
separately and is included in the price of the book.**

C000182307

Having purchased this book, you have access to the following online study materials:

CONTENT	AAT	
	Text	Kit
Electronic version of the book	✓	✓
Progress tests with instant answers	✓	
Mock assessments online	✓	✓
Material updates	✓	✓

How to access your online resources

Kaplan Financial students will already have a MyKaplan account and these extra resources will be available to you online. You do not need to register again, as this process was completed when you enrolled. If you are having problems accessing online materials, please ask your course administrator.

If you are not studying with Kaplan and did not purchase your book via a Kaplan website, to unlock your extra online resources please go to www.mykaplan.co.uk/addabook (even if you have set up an account and registered books previously). You will then need to enter the ISBN number (on the title page and back cover) and the unique pass key number contained in the scratch panel below to gain access. You will also be required to enter additional information during this process to set up or confirm your account details.

If you purchased through the Kaplan Publishing website you will automatically receive an e-mail invitation to MyKaplan. Please register your details using this email to gain access to your content. If you do not receive the e-mail or book content, please contact Kaplan Publishing.

Your Code and Information

This code can only be used once for the registration of one book online. This registration and your online content will expire when the final sittings for the examinations covered by this book have taken place. Please allow one hour from the time you submit your book details for us to process your request.

Please scratch the film to access your unique code.

Please be aware that this code is case-sensitive and you will need to include the dashes within the passcode, but not when entering the ISBN.

PUBLISHING

AAT

AQ2016

ADVANCED DIPLOMA IN ACCOUNTING

Synoptic Assessment

EXAM KIT

This Exam Kit supports study for the following AAT qualifications:

AAT Advanced Diploma in Accounting – Level 3

AAT Advanced Certificate in Bookkeeping – Level 3

AAT Advanced Diploma in Accounting at SCQF – Level 6

British Library Cataloguing-in-Publication Data

A catalogue record for this book is available from the British Library.

Published by:

Kaplan Publishing UK

Unit 2 The Business Centre

Molly Millar's Lane

Wokingham

Berkshire

RG41 2QZ

ISBN: 978-1-83996-091-8

© Kaplan Financial Limited, 2021

Printed and bound in Great Britain.

This Product includes content from the International Ethics Standards Board for Accountants (IESBA), published by the International Federation of Accountants (IFAC) in 2015 and is used with permission of IFAC.

CONTENTS

Features in this exam kit

In addition to providing a wide ranging bank of real exam style questions, we have also included in this kit:

- unit-specific information and advice on exam technique

- our recommended approach to make your revision for this particular unit as effective as possible.

You will find a wealth of other resources to help you with your studies on the AAT website:

www.aat.org.uk/

Quality and accuracy are of the utmost importance to us so if you spot an error in any of our products, please send an email to mykaplanreporting@kaplan.com with full details, or follow the link to the feedback form in MyKaplan.

Our Quality Co-ordinator will work with our technical team to verify the error and take action to ensure it is corrected in future editions.

SYNOPTIC ASSESSMENT

AAT AQ16 introduces a Synoptic Assessment, which students must complete if they are to achieve the appropriate qualification upon completion of a qualification. In the case of the Advanced Diploma in Accounting, students must pass all of the mandatory assessments and the Synoptic Assessment to achieve the qualification.

As a Synoptic Assessment is attempted following completion of individual units, it draws upon knowledge and understanding from those units. It may be appropriate for students to retain their study materials for individual units until they have successfully completed the Synoptic Assessment for that qualification.

All units within the Advanced Diploma in Accounting are mandatory. Four units are assessed individually in end of unit assessments, but this qualification also includes a synoptic assessment, sat towards the end of the qualification, which draws on and assesses knowledge and understanding from across the qualification:

- Advanced Bookkeeping – end of unit assessment
- Final Accounts Preparation – end of unit assessment
- Management Accounting: Costing – end of unit assessment
- Ethics for accountants – assessed within the synoptic assessment only

Summary of learning outcomes from underlying units which are assessed in the synoptic assessment

Underlying unit	Learning outcomes required
Advanced Bookkeeping	LO1, LO2, LO3, LO4, LO5
Final Accounts Preparation	LO1, LO2, LO3, LO4, LO5, LO6
Management Accounting: Costing	LO1, LO2, LO3, LO4, LO5
Ethics for Accountants	LO1, LO2, LO3, LO4, LO5

FORMAT OF THE ASSESSMENT

The sample synoptic assessment comprises seven tasks and covers all six assessment objectives. Students will be assessed by computer-based assessment. Marking of the assessment is partially by computer and partially human marked.

In any one assessment, students may not be assessed on all content, or on the full depth or breadth of a piece of content. The content assessed may change over time to ensure validity of assessment, but all assessment criteria will be tested over time.

The following weighting is based upon the AAT Qualification Specification documentation which may be subject to variation.

	Assessment objective	Weighting
AO1	Demonstrate an understanding of the relevance of the ethical code for accountants, the need to act ethically in a given situation, and the appropriate action to take in reporting questionable behaviour	19%
AO2	Prepare accounting and respond to errors, omissions and other concerns, in accordance with accounting and ethical principles and relevant regulations	15%
AO3	Demonstrate an understanding of the inter-relationship between the financial accounting and management accounting systems of an organisation and how they can be used to support managers in decision making	16%
AO4	Apply ethical and accounting principles when preparing final accounts for different types of organisation, develop ethical courses of action and communicate relevant information effectively	19%
AO5	Analyse, interpret and report management accounting data.	15%
AO6	Prepare financial accounting information, comprising extended trial balances and final accounts for sole traders and partnerships.	16%
	Total	100%

Time allowed: 2 hours 30 minutes

PASS MARK: The pass mark for all AAT assessments is 70%.

 Always keep your eye on the clock and make sure you attempt all questions!

The detailed syllabus and study guide written by the AAT can be found at:

www.aat.org.uk/

ASSESSMENT OBJECTIVES

To perform this synoptic assessment effectively you need to know and understand the following:

Assessment objective 1	Demonstrate an understanding of the relevance of the ethical code for accountants, the need to act ethically in a given situation, and the appropriate action to take in reporting questionable behaviour
Related learning objectives	**Ethics for Accountants** LO1 Understand the need to act ethically LO2 Understand the relevance to the accountant's work of the ethical code for professional accountants LO4 Identify action to take in relation to unethical behaviour or illegal acts
Assessment objective 2	Prepare accounting records and respond to errors, omissions and other concerns, in accordance with accounting and ethical principles and relevant regulations
Related learning objectives	**Ethics for Accountants** LO3 Recognise how to act ethically in an accounting role LO4 Identify action to take in relation to unethical behaviour or illegal acts **Advanced Bookkeeping** LO1 Apply the principles of advanced double-entry bookkeeping LO2 Implement procedures for the acquisition and disposal of non-current assets LO3 Prepare and record depreciation calculations LO4 Record period end adjustments **Final Accounts Preparation** LO2 Explain the need for final accounts and the accounting and ethical principles underlying their preparation LO3 Prepare accounting records from incomplete information
Assessment objective 3	Demonstrate an understanding of the inter-relationship between the financial accounting and management accounting systems of an organisation and how they can be used to support managers in decision making
Related learning objectives	**Advanced Bookkeeping** LO3 Prepare and record depreciation calculations LO4 Record period end adjustments **Final Accounts Preparation** LO2 Explain the need for final accounts and the accounting and ethical principles underlying their preparation LO3 Prepare accounting records from incomplete information **Management Accounting: Costing** LO1 Understand the purpose and use of management accounting within an organisation

	LO2 Apply techniques required for dealing with costs
	LO3 Apportion costs according to organisational requirements
	LO5 Apply management accounting techniques to support decision making
Assessment objective 4	Apply ethical and accounting principles when preparing final accounts for different types of organisation, develop ethical courses of action and communicate relevant information effectively
Related learning objectives	**Ethics for Accountants** LO3 Recognise how to act ethically in an accounting role **Final Accounts Preparation** LO1 Distinguish between the financial recording and reporting requirements of different types of organisation LO2 Explain the need for final accounts and the accounting and ethical principles underlying their preparation LO3 Prepare accounting records from incomplete information LO4 Produce accounts for sole traders LO5 Produce accounts for partnerships LO6 Recognise the key differences between preparing accounts for a limited company and a sole trader
Assessment objective 5	Analyse, interpret and report management accounting data
Related learning objectives	**Management Accounting: Costing** LO1 Understand the purpose and use of management accounting within an organisation LO3 Apportion costs according to organisational requirements LO4 Analyse and review deviations from budget and report these to management LO5 Apply management accounting techniques to support decision making
Assessment objective 6	Prepare financial accounting information, comprising extended trial balances and final accounts for sole traders and partnerships
Related learning objectives	**Advanced Bookkeeping** LO5 Produce and extend the trial balance **Final Accounts Preparation** LO4 Produce accounts for sole traders LO5 Produce accounts for partnerships

INDEX TO QUESTIONS AND ANSWERS

KAPLAN PUBLISHING

EXAM TECHNIQUE

- **Do not skip any of the material** in the syllabus.

- **Read each question** *very* carefully.

- **Double-check your answer** before committing yourself to it.

- Answer **every** question – if you do not know an answer to a multiple choice question or true/false question, you don't lose anything by guessing. Think carefully before you **guess**.

- If you are answering a multiple-choice question, **eliminate first those answers that you know are wrong.** Then choose the most appropriate answer from those that are left.

- **Don't panic** if you realise you've answered a question incorrectly. Getting one question wrong will not mean the difference between passing and failing.

Computer-based exams – tips

- Do not attempt a CBA until you have **completed all study material** relating to it.

- On the AAT website there is a CBA demonstration. It is **ESSENTIAL** that you attempt this before your real CBA. You will become familiar with how to move around the CBA screens and the way that questions are formatted, increasing your confidence and speed in the actual exam.

- Be sure you understand how to use the **software** before you start the exam. If in doubt, ask the assessment centre staff to explain it to you.

- Questions are **displayed on the screen** and answers are entered using keyboard and mouse. At the end of the exam, in the case of those units not subject to human marking, you are given a certificate showing the result you have achieved.

- In addition to the traditional multiple-choice question type, CBAs will also contain **other types of questions**, such as number entry questions, drag and drop, true/false, pick lists or drop down menus or hybrids of these.

- In some CBAs you will have to type in complete computations or written answers.

- You need to be sure you **know how to answer questions** of this type before you sit the exam, through practice.

KAPLAN PUBLISHING

KAPLAN'S RECOMMENDED REVISION APPROACH

QUESTION PRACTICE IS THE KEY TO SUCCESS

Success in professional examinations relies upon you acquiring a firm grasp of the required knowledge at the tuition phase. In order to be able to do the questions, knowledge is essential.

However, the difference between success and failure often hinges on your exam technique on the day and making the most of the revision phase of your studies.

The **Kaplan Study Text** is the starting point, designed to provide the underpinning knowledge to tackle all questions. However, in the revision phase, poring over text books is not the answer.

Kaplan Pocket Notes are designed to help you quickly revise a topic area; however you then need to practise questions. There is a need to progress to exam style questions as soon as possible, and to tie your exam technique and technical knowledge together.

The importance of question practice cannot be over-emphasised.

The recommended approach below is designed by expert tutors in the field, in conjunction with their knowledge of the examiner and the specimen assessment.

You need to practise as many questions as possible in the time you have left.

OUR AIM

Our aim is to get you to the stage where you can attempt exam questions confidently, to time, in a closed book environment, with no supplementary help (i.e. to simulate the real examination experience).

Practising your exam technique is also vitally important for you to assess your progress and identify areas of weakness that may need more attention in the final run up to the examination.

In order to achieve this we recognise that initially you may feel the need to practice some questions with open book help.

Good exam technique is vital.

THE KAPLAN REVISION PLAN

Stage 1: Assess areas of strengths and weaknesses

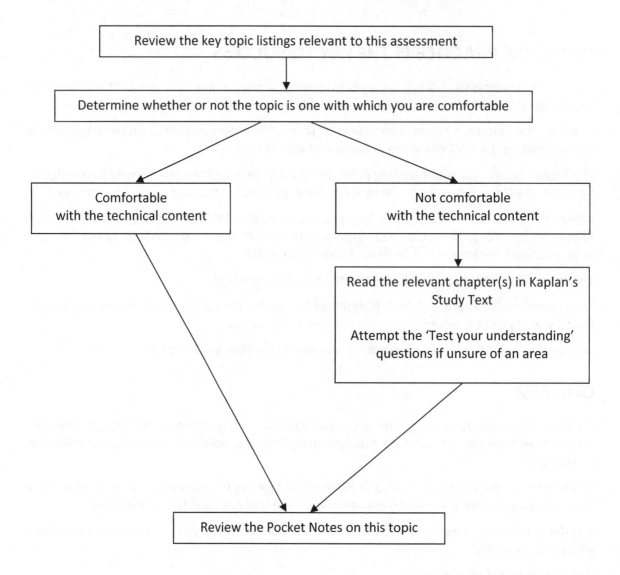

Stage 2: Practice questions

Follow the order of revision of topics as presented in this Kit and attempt the questions in the order suggested.

Try to avoid referring to Study Texts and your notes and the model answer until you have completed your attempt.

Review your attempt with the model answer and assess how much of the answer you achieved.

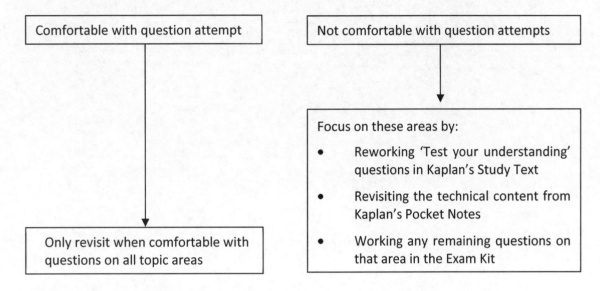

Comfortable with question attempt

Not comfortable with question attempts

Only revisit when comfortable with questions on all topic areas

Focus on these areas by:

*   Reworking 'Test your understanding' questions in Kaplan's Study Text

*   Revisiting the technical content from Kaplan's Pocket Notes

*   Working any remaining questions on that area in the Exam Kit

Stage 3: Final pre-exam revision

We recommend that you **attempt at least one mock examination** containing a set of previously unseen exam-standard questions.

Attempt the mock CBA online in timed, closed book conditions to simulate the real exam experience.

Section 1

PRACTICE QUESTIONS

TASK 1 COMPUTER ASSESSED

Assessment objective 1	Demonstrate an understanding of the relevance of the ethical code for accountants, the need to act ethically in a given situation, and the appropriate action to take in reporting questionable behaviour.

1   CODE OF ETHICS

Indicate whether the following statements are true or false.

	True	False
An accountant is under no duty to disclose the limitations of their expertise to the client		
An accountant is only responsible for his or her own professional qualifications and training		
An accountant may need to compromise the most precise attention to detail in preparing work in order to meet a reasonable deadline		

2   INTEGRITY

Is an accountant breaching their duty of integrity if they: (tick all that apply)

Give responsibility to a client to discover important information that is freely available?	
Only tells the client the information they have specifically asked for or that is habitually provided?	
Forgets to mention something important?	
Withholds information that may be compromising for the employer?	

3   CONFIDENTIAL

When might it be appropriate for an accountant to disclose information, provided in confidence?

A   At the request of the client

B   At the request of the regulator

C   At the request of a solicitor

D   At the request of the employer

4   THREATS

Classify the following threats according to the situations:

Self-interest threats	Preparing accounts for a campaign group of which the accountant is a leading member
Self-review threats	Preparing accounts under an unrealistically imposed deadline by a major client
Advocacy threats	Preparing accounts for your close relative's business
Familiarity threats	Preparing accounts for your spouse's business
Intimidation threats	Preparing accounts and providing a basic audit function on those accounts

5   E

E, a trainee management accountant, prepares an annual analysis of the performance of all staff, including their own. The analysis is used by the financial director to calculate staff bonuses each year.

According to the Code of Professional Ethics which of the threats listed below would apply to E?

A   Advocacy threat

B   Intimidation threat

C   Familiarity threat

D   Self-interest threat

6   R

R, a trainee management accountant is employed by JH. R has prepared the draft annual financial statements for JH and presented them to JH's Chief Executive prior to the executive board meeting. The Chief Executive has told R that the profit reported in the financial statements is too low and must be increased by £500,000 before the financial statements can be approved by the executive board.

Which of the threats listed below would apply to R in this situation, according to the Code of Professional Ethics?

A   Advocacy threat

B   Self-review threat

C   Intimidation threat

D   Self-interest threat

7   CX

CX, a professional accountant is facing a dilemma. CX is working on the preparation of a long term profit forecast required by the local stock market listing regulations.

At a previous management board meeting, the projections had been criticised by board members as being too pessimistic. CX was asked to review the assumptions and increase the profit projections.

CX revised the assumptions, but this had only marginally increased the forecast profits.

At yesterday's board meeting the board members had discussed the assumptions and specified new values to be used to prepare a revised forecast. In CX's view the new values grossly overestimate the forecast profits.

The management board intends to publish the revised forecasts.

(a)   Which TWO of the following ethical principles does CX face?

A   Integrity

B   Confidentiality

C   Professional care and due competence

D   Objectivity

E   Professional behaviour

(b) **Place the following options into the highlighted boxes in the table below to correctly show the order CX should deal with an ethical dilemma.**

| Report internally to immediate management |
| Report externally |
| Remove themselve from the situation |
| Gather evidence and document the problem |
| Report internally to higher management |

	Dealing with an ethical dilemma
1	
2	
3	
4	
5	

8 PRINCIPLES

Match the principles from the Code of Professional Ethics in the list below to the relevant interpretation:

- Confidentiality
- Integrity
- Professional behaviour
- Professional competence and due care
- Objectivity

Principle	Interpretation
	Maintaining a relevant level of professional knowledge and skills so that a competent service can be provided.
	Complying with relevant laws and regulations.
	Being straightforward, honest and truthful in all professional and business relationships.
	Not disclosing information unless there is specific permission or a legal or professional duty to do so.
	Not allowing bias, conflict of interest or the influence of other people to override professional judgement.

9 ACTION

You are a management accountant working a UK listed chemical company. During the course of your duties, you become aware that the company is dumping waste illegally. You have raised this with your manager who has told you to ignore the issue.

Which of the following is NOT an appropriate course of action to take next?

A   Contacting AAT's ethical helpline for advice

B   Reporting the company to the environment agency

C   Contacting a journalist at a national newspaper

D   Taking the matter to the Audit committee

10 FUNDAMENTAL PRINCIPLES

The AAT Code of Ethics contains five fundamental principles of professional ethics for management accountants. Which of the following are fundamental principles, according to the Code? (Select ALL correct answers)

Confidentiality	
Honesty	
Objectivity	
Respect	
Integrity	

11 ETHICS AND LAW

Which of the following statement/s is/are correct?

If a person complies with the letter of the law that person will always be acting ethically.	
Ethics in business is the application of ethical values to business.	
If a company has a code of ethics this will eliminate the need for legislation.	

12 ISSUES

Which of the following relates to an ethical issue?

A   The introduction of new IT systems to ensure the confidentiality of customers.

B   The recruitment of a new, highly qualified, finance director.

C   The purchase of larger more centrally located business premises to facilitate the expansion of the business.

D   The introduction of monthly reporting systems to maximise efficiency.

13   BREACHES

Which of the following statements are true?

You have been told that one of your colleagues in the accounts department has regularly submitted inflated expenses claims. This is a breach of the fundamental principle of objectivity.	
You are aware that a colleague in the accounts department regularly takes home reports to check and does so after a few cocktails. This is a breach of the fundamental principle of professional behaviour.	
You are employed as Management Accountant and have been asked to dismiss one of your colleagues for misconduct. You are aware that this is untrue and that the Company is trying to reduce the workforce without making the due redundancy payments. This is a breach of the fundamental principle of integrity.	

TASK 2 COMPUTER ASSESSED

Assessment objective 2	Prepare accounting and respond to errors, omissions and other concerns, in accordance with accounting and ethical principles and relevant regulations.

14   PIXIE PAPERS

A supply of paper has been delivered to Alpha Ltd by Pixie Paper.

Pixie Paper

24 Eden Terrace, Durham, DH9 7TE

VAT Registration No. 464 392 401

Invoice No. 1679

Alpha Ltd

121 Baker St

Newcastle, NE1 7DJ

9 Aug 20XX

50 boxes of A4 paper, product code 16257 @ £10 each	£500
VAT	£0
Total	£500

Terms: 30 days net

Has the correct net price been calculated?	Y	N
Has the total invoice price been calculated correctly?	Y	N
What would be the VAT amount charged if the invoice was correct?	£_____	
What would be the total amount charged if the invoice was correct?	£_____	

15   PAINTS R US

A supply of paint has been delivered to Painting Supplies Ltd by Paints R Us.

Paints R Us

19 Valley Gardens, Stanley, DH5 8JJ

VAT Registration No. 421 385 602

Invoice No. 2485

Painting Supplies Ltd

19 Edmund St

Newcastle, NE6 5DJ

10 Feb 20XX

20 tins of blue paint, product code 23567 @ £8 each	£160.00
VAT	£32.00
Total	£192.00

Terms: 30 days net

Check the invoice against the purchase order and answer the following questions.

Has the correct net price been calculated?	Y	N
Has the total invoice price been calculated correctly?	Y	N
What would be the VAT amount charged if the invoice was correct?	£_____	
What would be the total amount charged if the invoice was correct?	£_____	

16   MONT

Mont is a VAT (sales tax) registered trader and all of the sales and purchases are standard rated for VAT (sales tax) purposes. They have entered the following transactions:

(i)   sales for cash of £2,200 plus VAT

(ii)   purchases on credit for £1,800 including VAT

(iii)   sales on credit for £3,840 including VAT

(iv)   purchases for cash for £1,400 plus VAT

Task

(a) Write up the ledger accounts to reflect these transactions and balance off the VAT account.

Sales account

	£		£
		Bank	
		Receivables	

Bank account

	£		£
Sales/VAT (sales tax)		Purchases/VAT (sales tax)	

Receivables account

	£		£
Sales/VAT (sales tax)			

VAT (sales tax) account

	£		£
Payables		Bank	
Bank		Receivables	
Balance c/d			
	――		――
	――		――
		Balance b/d	

Purchases account

	£		£
Payables			
Bank			

Payables account

	£		£
		Purchases/VAT (sales tax)	

(b) What does the balance on the VAT (sales tax) account represent (*delete as appropriate)?

The **credit/debit*** balance remaining on the VAT (sales tax) account is the amount of VAT (sales tax) owed **to/by*** the tax authorities (HM Revenue and Customs).

17   BESS

Bess proves the accuracy of her sales and purchases ledgers by preparing monthly control accounts. At 1 September 20X7 the following balances existed in the business records, and the control accounts agreed.

	Debit	Credit
	£	£
Sales ledger control account	188,360	2,140
Purchases ledger control account	120	89,410

The following are the totals of transactions which took place during September 20X7, as extracted from the business records.

	£
Credit sales	101,260
Credit purchases	68,420
Sales returns	9,160
Purchases returns	4,280
Cash received from customers	91,270
Cash paid to suppliers	71,840
Cash discounts allowed	1,430
Cash discounts received	880
Irrecoverable debts written off	460
Refunds to customers	300
Contra settlements	480

At 30 September 20X7 the balances in the sales and purchases ledgers, as extracted, totalled:

	Debit	Credit
	£	£
Sales ledger balances	To be ascertained	3,360
Purchases ledger balances	90	To be ascertained

An initial attempt to balance the two ledgers showed that neither of them agreed.

The differences were found to be due to the following.

(i)   A contra settlement of £500 had not been included in the totals of transactions prepared for the control accounts.

(ii)   A new employee had mistakenly entered five copy sales invoices into the purchases day book as if they had been purchases invoices and entered the amounts to new purchases ledger accounts. The total of these invoices was £1,360.

(iii)   A £20 cash refund to a customer was made out of petty cash, and has not been included in the summary of transactions given above. The £20 was entered to the sales ledger as if it had been a cash receipt from the customer, and this resulted in a £40 credit balance on the account, which was still outstanding at 30 September 20X7.

When these errors had been corrected both control accounts agreed with the ledgers.

Prepare the sales ledger and purchases ledger control accounts for the month of September 20X7 after these errors had been corrected, and hence ascertain the missing totals of the ledger balances as indicated above.

Sales ledger control account

20X7		£	20X7		£
01 Sep	Balance b/d		01 Sep	Balance b/d	
30 Sep	Sales		30 Sep	Sales returns	
	Cash refunds			Cash received	
	Petty cash refund			Cash discounts	
	Balance c/d			Irrecoverable debts	
				Contras	
				Balance c/d	
		———			———
		———			———

Purchases ledger control account

20X7		£	20X7		£
01 Sep	Balance b/d		01 Sep	Balance b/d	
30 Sep	Purchases returns		30 Sep	Purchases	
	Cash to suppliers			Balance c/d	
	Cash discounts				
	Contras				
	Balance c/d				
		———			———
		———			———

18 SALLY

At 31 December 20X7 the totals of the subsidiary (sales) ledger balances of a sole trader were as follows.

£

Sales ledger control account   debit   384,600

After reviewing these balances in preparing the financial statements for the year ended 31 December 20X7, a number of adjustments are necessary.

(i)   A contra settlement had been agreed during the year offsetting an amount due from Sally Limited in the sales ledger of £1,080 against the balance due to that company in the purchases ledger. No entry had been made for this contra.

(ii)   The following debts due from sales ledger customers are to be written off.

Customer	£
P	840
Q	120
R	360
S	2,090
T	180

(iii)   The allowance for doubtful debts, which stood at £3,060 is to be increased to £5,200.

(iv)   During the year £200 cash received from AUT Limited had mistakenly been entered into the account of AUE Limited in the sales ledger.

Task

(a)   Prepare journal entries to give effect to adjustments (i) to (iv).

		Dr	Cr
		£	£
(i)	Sally Ltd purchase ledger control		
	Sally Ltd sales ledger control		

(ii)	Irrecoverable debts expense		
	Sales ledger control		

(iii)	Allowance for doubtful debts adjustment		
	Allowance for doubtful debts		

(iv)	AUE Ltd sales ledger		
	AUT Ltd sales ledger		

(b)   Calculate the amounts which should appear in the Statement of Financial Position as at 31 December 20X7 for receivables.

£

19   GEORGE

George has fixtures and fittings which were originally purchased on 1 May 20X0 for £8,400. These fixtures and fittings were sold on 1 December 20X1 for £6,000 having been depreciated at 15% straight line.

Task

(a)   What would be the carrying amount of the fixtures and fittings on the date of disposal if the depreciation is calculated on a monthly basis?

£

(b)   What would be the amount of profit or loss on disposal of the fixtures and fittings?

(Circle the correct answer for gain or loss)

Gain/Loss

£

20   MATTRESS

Daniel James is the proprietor of Mattress, a business which buys and sells bedroom furniture.

- The year end is 31 May 20X1.

- You are employed to assist with the book-keeping.

- The business currently operates a manual system consisting of a general ledger, a sales ledger and a purchases ledger.

- Double entry takes place in the general ledger. Individual accounts of receivables and payables are kept in memorandum accounts.

- You use a purchases day book, a sales day book, a purchases returns day book and a sales returns day book. Totals from the day books are transferred into the general ledger.

At the end of the financial year on 31 May 20X1, the balances were extracted from the general ledger and entered into an extended trial balance.

It was found that the total of the debit column of the trial balance did not agree with the total of the credit column. The difference was posted to a suspense account.

After the preparation of the extended trial balance the following errors were found:

(a)   Motor expenses of £150 were debited to the Motor Vehicles at cost account. Ignore depreciation.

(b)   The VAT (sales tax) column in the purchases returns day book was undercast by £400.

(c)   On 31 May 20X1 some of the fixtures and fittings were sold. The original cost of the assets was £11,000 and they were bought on 1 June 19W9. Depreciation provision to the date of disposal was made in the accounts and this totalled £4,400 for these fixtures and fittings. The disposal proceeds were £7,000. This money was correctly entered in the bank account, but no other entry was made.

(d)   Sales of £9,500 were entered into the sales account as £5,900. All other entries were correct.

(e)   A wages payment of £1,255 was debited to both the wages account and the bank account.

Task 1

Prepare journal entries to record the correction of the errors. Dates and narratives are not required.

Account		Dr	Cr
		£	£
(a)	Motor expenses		
	Motor vehicle at cost		
(b)	Suspense		
	VAT (sales tax) account		
(c)	Disposal account		
	Fixtures and fittings at cost		
	Accumulated depreciation (F&F)		
	Disposal account		
	Suspense		
	Disposal account		
	Disposal account		
	Statement of profit or loss account (gain)		
(d)	Suspense		
	Sales		
(e)	Suspense		
	Bank		

21 NCA1

NCA1 Limited is not registered for VAT and has a year end of 31 December 20X0.

The following is a purchase invoice received by NCA1 Limited:

Invoice # 212532		
To: NCA1 Limited	Graham's Garages	**Date:** 28 November X0
428 Hoole Road	32 Oldfield Way	
Chester	Chester	
CH4 GFV	CH12 RTH	
		£
Vauxhall Van	Registration number ES54 DCS	15,000.00
Delivery		250.00
Tax Disc		210.00
Less part exchange	Registration number FD01 VBA	(3,800.00)
Amount due		11,660.00
Settlement terms: Strictly 60 days		

The following information relates to the vehicle that was part exchanged:

Registration number	FD01 VBA
Length of ownership	4 years 2 months
Purchase price	£12,000.00

- Vehicles are depreciated at 30% on a reducing balance basis.

- Non-current assets are depreciated in the year of acquisition but not in the year of disposal.

You now need to complete the journal to reflect the purchase of the new van and the part exchange of the old van.

Account	Dr	Cr
Disposals		
Motor vehicles at cost		

Motor vehicles accumulated depreciation		
Disposals		

Motor vehicles at cost		
Motor vehicle expenses		
Disposals		
Sundry payables		
Totals		

22 DAVE'S DOORS

- Dave's Doors is a sole trader business that is registered for VAT at the standard rate of 20%. His year end is 31/12/X4.

- During 20X4, machine 'A' was sold, for total proceeds of £10,000 (cheque received).

- Machine 'A' was acquired on 01/07/X1 at a cost of £20,000 (excluding VAT).

- The depreciation policy for machinery is 10% per annum on a reducing balance basis. Non-current assets are depreciated in full in the year of acquisition but not in the year of disposal.

(a) What is the accumulated depreciation of machine 'A' in the year of disposal?

£

(b)   Complete the journal to reflect the disposal of machine 'A'. A picklist of account names has been provided below. You are able to use an account name more than once. More rows than required have been provided below.

Account	Dr	Cr
Disposals account		
Machinery cost account		

Machinery accumulated depreciation account		
Disposals account		

Bank		
VAT Control		
Disposals account		
Totals		

(c)   What was the profit or loss made on disposal?

£

23   JP BAKERY

You are employed by Jane Parker who is a baker. You are her bookkeeper and she has asked you to create a trial balance. Below are the balances extracted from the main ledger at 30 April 20X2.

(a)   Enter the balances into the columns of the trial balance provided below. Total the two columns and enter an appropriate suspense account balance to ensure that the two totals agree.

	£	Debit	Credit
Accruals	4,820		
Prepayments	2,945		
Motor expenses	572		
Admin expenses	481		
Light and Heat	1,073		
Revenue	48,729		
Purchases	26,209		
SLCA	5,407		
PLCA	3,090		
Rent	45		
Purchase returns	306		

	£	**Debit**	**Credit**
Discounts allowed	567		
Capital	10,000		
Loan	15,000		
Interest paid	750		
Drawings	4,770		
Motor vehicles – cost	19,000		
Motor vehicle – accumulated depreciation	2,043		
VAT control owing	2,995		
Wages	20,000		
Suspense account			
Totals			

(b) Since the trial balance has been produced you have noticed a number of errors which are as follows:

(i) Jane put £5,000 into the business after receiving a large cheque as a Christmas present from her father. This has been put through the bank account but no other entries have been made.

(ii) The Gross column of the SDB has been overcast by £385.

(iii) The VAT column of the PDB has been undercast by £193.

(iv) An amount of £4,500 paid for rent has been credited to both the rent account and the bank account.

(v) An accrual for electricity at the year end of £1,356 has been correctly credited to the accruals account but no other entry has been made.

Prepare the entries to correct these errors using the blank journal below. Dates and narratives are not required.

		Dr **£**	**Cr**
(i)	Suspense		
	Capital		
(ii)	Suspense		
	Sales ledger control account		
(iii)	VAT		
	Suspense		

(iv)	Rent		
	Suspense		
(v)	Electricity		
	Suspense		

24 CONTROL LTD

You are working on the accounts of Control Ltd for the year ended 30 September 20X6. You have the following information:

Sales for the year ended 30 September 20X6

- Credit sales amounted to £46,000 net of sales tax

- Cash sales amounted to £212,000 net of sales tax

- All sales are standard rated for sales tax at 20%.

Payments from the bank account for the year ended 30 September 20X6

- Payroll expenses   £48,000
- Administration expenses   £6,400 ignore sales tax
- Vehicle running costs   £192,000 including sales tax at 20%
- Drawings   £41,800
- Sales tax   £17,300

Summary of balances available

Balance as at	30 September 20X5	30 September 20X6
Bank account	5,630	8,140
Trade receivables	4,120	5,710
Sales tax (credit balances)	4,200	4,575

(a) Calculate the figure for credit sales for entry into the receivables (sales ledger) control account?

£_____

(b)   Using the figures given above (including your answer to part (a), prepare the sales ledger control account for the year ended 30 September 20X6, showing clearly the receipts paid into the bank as the balancing figure.

Receivables (Sales ledger) control account

Balance b/d		Bank	
Credit sales		Balance c/d	

(c)   Calculate the cash sales inclusive of sales tax which have been paid into the bank account. All cash sales are banked.

£_____

(d)   Show a summarised bank account for the year ended 30 September 20X6.

Bank account

Balance b/d		Payroll expenses	
SLCA		Administration expenses	
Cash sales		Vehicle running costs	
		Drawings	
		Sales tax	
		Balance c/d	

25   BRIAN

You are given the following information about a sole trader called Brian as at 31 March 20X2:

The value of assets and liabilities were:

- Non-current assets at carrying amount   £14,000
- Bank   £2,500
- Trade payables   £10,300
- Opening capital (at 1 April 20X1)   £3,700
- Drawings for the year   £1,500

There were no other assets or liabilities.

Calculate the profit for the year ended 30 March 20X2.

£_____

26 ELSIE

During the year ended 30 September 20X7, Elsie, a sole trader, made sales of £1,280,000 and made a sales margin of 25% on these. Rosemary made purchases of £970,200 during the year ended 30 September 20X7 and inventory was valued at £98,006 at the year end.

Using this information, complete the following:

(a) Calculate the cost of goods sold for the year ended 30 September 20X7.

£_____

(b) Calculate the value of the inventory at 1 October 20X6.

£_____

27 FIVE SCENARIOS

Consider the following scenarios.

Scenario 1

Alessandro is an AAT member in practice employed by Sueka LLP. He has acquired some information about Polina Ltd in the course of acting for the company on an assurance engagement.

Complete the following sentence by selecting the appropriate option from the three options given below.

'The principle of confidentiality imposes an obligation on Alessandro to refrain from

using the information to the advantage of Sueka LLP'	
disclosing the information within Sueka LLP'	
disclosing the information to anyone at Polina Ltd'	

Scenario 2

Jacob, an AAT member in practice, is conducting a second interview of an excellent candidate (also an AAT member) for a senior post in Jacob's firm. When discussing remuneration, the potential employee states she will bring a copy of the database of clients from her old firm to introduce new clients to Jacob's firm. She also says she knows a lot of negative information about her old firm which Jacob could use to gain clients from them.

Identify which of the following are the most appropriate actions for Jacob to take following the interview.

As she shows business acumen, offer her the job	
As she has breached the fundamental principles of integrity and confidentiality, report her to the AAT	
As she lacks integrity, inform her that she will not be offered the job	

Scenario 3

Vernon, a member in practice, performs book-keeping services for both Yen Ltd and Piston Ltd. The two companies are in dispute about a series of purchases that Yen Ltd made from Piston Ltd.

Identify which fundamental ethical principles are threatened here from the options below.

Objectivity and confidentiality	
Integrity and professional behaviour	
Confidentiality and professional competence	

Scenario 4

Nick is a member in business. His cousin Sam has recently been employed by an organisation with which Nick has regular business dealings. Sam's position means that she would be able to offer Nick preferential treatment in the awarding of major contracts.

What should Nick do?

Nothing	
Seek legal advice	
Advise Sam of relevant threats and safeguards that will protect Nick should he receive such an offer from Sam's organisation	
Immediately inform higher levels of management	

Scenario 5

Conner, a member in practice, has just received a call from a potential new client asking him to help in a business transaction. However, when asked for her address, the client said she would rather not say.

Advise Conner on how to respond to the client.

	Yes	No
Continue with forging a relationship with the client in the usual manner		
Inform the client that without knowing the correct address the client/ accountant relationship cannot be forged		
Consider reporting the conversation to NCA		

28 JESS

(a) Jessica, a member in practice, has been tasked to complete an important assignment. However, she knows that she will not have enough time complete the work properly.

Which fundamental principle is under threat?

Objectivity	
Integrity	
Confidentiality	
Professional behaviour	
Professional competence and due care	

(b) Beverley, a qualified AAT member in practice, has been asked to complete a tax assignment involving some complex Inheritance Tax calculations, which Beverley does not feel confident she fully understands.

Should Beverley should undertake the assignment?

Yes	
No	

29 NIGHT OUT

Bella, a professional accountant, was invited on a 'night out' with others from the accounts department. This became quite a boisterous evening and it ended with the Finance Director removing a sign from the front of a shop which he brought into the office the next day as a reminder of the good evening.

Required:

(a) Which fundamental ethical principle the Finance Director has breached?

Objectivity	
Integrity	
Confidentiality	
Professional behaviour	
Professional competence and due care	

(b) What course of action Bella should take?

Nothing	
Report the FD to the police	
Immediately inform the Managing Director	
Suggest to the Finance Director that the sign should be replaced, and possibly discuss the matter with the Managing Director	

30 RS

RS, an employee, prepares monthly management accounting information for XYZ which includes detailed performance data that is used to calculate staff bonuses. Based on information prepared by RS this year's bonuses will be lower than expected.

RS has had approaches from other staff offering various incentives to make accruals for additional revenue and other reversible adjustments, to enable all staff (including RS) to receive increased or higher bonuses.

(a)   **Which TWO of the following ethical principles does RS face?**

        A   Integrity

        B   Confidentiality

        C   Professional care and due competence

        D   Objectivity

        E   Professional behaviour

(b)   **Which of the following ethical threats does RS face?**

        A   Advocacy threat

        B   Self-review threat

        C   Intimidation threat

        D   Self-interest threat

TASK 3 HUMAN ASSESSED

Assessment objective 3	Demonstrate an understanding of the inter-relationship between the financial accounting and management accounting systems of an organisation and how they can be used to support managers in decision making

31 INVENTORY

The inventory record for component XYZ for the month of January showed:

	Receipts	Value £	Issues
Opening inventory	500	1,250	
4 January	1,000	2,750	
11 January	1,600	4,480	
18 January	1,200	3,480	
19 January			2,100
25 January	1,500	4,350	
31 January			1,800

(a) Calculate the cost of issues during the month using the FIFO method of pricing issues.

(b) Calculate the value of inventory at 31 January using the LIFO method of pricing issues.

(c) Calculate the price at which the issues on 31 January would be made using the average cost method of pricing.

(d) Describe how the different methods used to cost the inventory can have an effect on the profit for the period.

32 LABOUR – OVERTIME

Explain how overtime is treated as direct and indirect labour in the management accounts of a business.

33 AC V ABC

The ABC Company manufactures two products, Product Alpha and Product Beta. Both are produced in a very labour-intensive environment and use similar processes. Alpha and Beta differ by volume. Beta is a high-volume product, while Alpha is a low-volume product. Details of product inputs, outputs and the costs of activities are as follows:

	Direct labour hours/unit	Annual output (units)	Number of purchase orders	Number of set-ups
Alpha	5	1,200	70	40
Beta	5	10,800	80	60
			150	100

Fixed overhead costs amount to a total of £420,000 and have been analysed as follows:

	£
Labour-related	90,000
Purchasing related	150,000
Set-up related	180,000

(a) Using a traditional method of overhead absorption based on labour hours, what is the overhead cost per unit for each unit of product Alpha?

(b) Explain what a cost pool and a cost driver are when using Activity based costing (ABC), calculations are not required.

(c) Discuss the pros and cons of using ABC as a method of absorbing overheads.

34   MC V AC

Animal Feeds Ltd has prepared a forecast for the next quarter for the production and sales of organic animal feed.

Animal Feeds Ltd budgets to produce 1,800 kg of the feed and sell 1,000 kg. The cost and revenue for this budget is as follows:

	£000
Sales	50,000
Direct materials	7,560
Direct labour	17,640
Fixed production overheads	3,600
Advertising (fixed cost)	2,010

Animal Feeds Ltd has no opening inventory of the feed.

Marginal costing

	£000	£000
Sales		50,000
Opening inventory	0	
Production costs	25,200	
Closing inventory	11,200	
Cost of sales		14,000
Contribution		36,000
Fixed costs		5,610
Profit for the period		30,390

Absorption costing

	£000	£000
Sales		50,000
Opening inventory	0	
Production costs	28,800	
Closing inventory	12,800	
Cost of sales		16,000
Gross Profit		34,000
Non-production cost		2,010
Profit for the period		31,990

Required:

Explain why the profits are different when using marginal and absorption costing.

35 CVP

Dilemma makes a product that is aimed at the teenage leisure market in the UK. After a number of successful years, they are considering whether to expand their production capability by a factor of 50% to take advantage of rising demand. The accountant has produced the following information:

1   Current sales per year – 500,000 units at £1.70 per unit.

2   Variable costs £1.40 per unit.

3   Fixed costs £96,000 per year.

4   If production is increased it is anticipated that:

    (i)   fixed costs will increase by £34,000

    (ii)   variable costs are expected to fall by £0.05 per unit due to bulk purchasing of raw material

    (iii)   the selling price is expected to be reduced by £0.10 per unit for all units.

At a recent management meeting the following comments were noted:

1   The Production Director expressed concern at the revenue projections. In his opinion there are a number of risks inherent in the new strategy. His main concern is that the total number of teenagers is falling, although he conceded that perhaps future teenagers may have more money to spend per head. He also asked if future changes in raw material prices and wage rates had been fully taken into account.

2   The Sales Director stated that she felt much more confident about the plan and said that sales had been rising for some time and, in her opinion, the number of teenagers is increasing. She also thought that inflation should not be too much of a problem.

Required:

(a) For both the present and proposed situations calculate:

(i) the breakeven point in units and sales revenue

(ii) the annual profit

(iii) the margin of safety ratio.

(b) On the basis of your answers to part (a), state, with reasons, what your advice would be to Dilemma.

36 LF

(a) X manufactures four liquids – A, B, C and D. The selling price and unit cost details for these products are as follows:

	A	B	C	D
	£/litre	£/litre	£/litre	£/litre
Selling price	100	110	120	120
Direct materials	24	30	16	21
Direct labour (£6/hour)	18	15	24	27
Direct expenses	–	–	3	–
Variable overhead	12	10	16	18
Fixed overhead **Note 1**	24	20	32	36
Profit	22	35	29	18

Note 1:

Fixed overhead is absorbed on the basis of labour hours, based on a budget of 1,600 hours per quarter.

During the next three months the number of direct labour hours is expected to be limited to 1,345. The same labour is used for all products.

The marketing director has identified the maximum demand for each of the four products during the next three months as follows:

A   200 litres

B   150 litres

C   100 litres

D   120 litres

(a) Determine the number of litres of products A, B, C and D to be produced/sold in the next three months in order to maximise profits, and calculate the profit that this would yield.

(b) Explain the calculation

37 FLEXED BUDGETS

Stinger has prepared a forecast for the next quarter for one of its products, the Ouch. The forecast is based on selling and producing 2,160 units.

	£
Sales revenue	64,800
Direct materials	9,720
Direct labour	22,680
Fixed overheads	12,960
Semi-variable costs	6,804
Total cost	52,164
Total profit	12,636
Profit per unit (to 2 decimal places)	5.85

Stinger has stated that if 5,400 units were produced the semi-variable cost will be £13,284.

(a)   Complete the table below to calculate the revenue, costs, profit and profit per unit if 2,700 units were produced.

	£
Sales revenue	
Direct materials	
Direct labour	
Overheads	
Semi-variable costs	
Total cost	
Total profit	
Profit per unit (to 2 decimal places)	

(b)   Explain, with references to cost behaviours, the theory behind your calculations.

(c)   Explain why the profit per unit changes.

38 VARIANCES

A manufacturing company has performed variance analysis on its costs from last month. The variances produced are:

Materials	2,000 Favourable
Labour	0
Fixed overheads	18,000 Favourable

There were some recent events that your manager would like you to consider when analysing these variances:

Storage facilities: alternatives storage facilities were rented at the beginning of last month leading to lower monthly payments.

Machinery: at the beginning of last month, an investment was made in more modern and efficient machinery which has a slightly smaller monthly depreciation cost.

Staff upgrade: The company had recruited skilled machine operators to operate the machinery at the start of last month but this had led to making the existing unskilled workers redundant at the same time. The unskilled workers had been notified of their redundancy three months ago.

Required:

Discuss how the variances could have been affected by the information above.

39 INVESTMENT APPRAISAL

Loft Lifting Ltd has four possible investment opportunities but is only able to invest in two.

- The first (1) investment needs to be risk limited
- The second (2) investment should provide the best return for the shareholders possible.

The investment opportunities produce the following forecasts.

Method	Option 1	Option 2	Option 3	Option 4
Payback (years)	3.0	4.0	3.3	3.9
Net present value (£000)	16	21	36	52

(a) **Which options Loft Lifting should invest in for each investment (tick one option for each investment)?**

Investment	Option 1	Option 2	Option 3	Option 4
1				
2				

(b) **Explain you answer to part (a)**

TASK 4 HUMAN ASSESSED

Assessment objective 4	Apply ethical and accounting principles when preparing final accounts for different types of organisation, develop ethical courses of action and communicate relevant information effectively

40   DILIGENCE

Conner, a member in practice, has just received a call from a potential new client asking Conner to help in a business transaction. However, when asked for his address, the client said he would rather not say.

Required:

(a)   **Advise Conner on how to respond to the client.**

(b)   **Explain what other action(s) Conner should take.**

41   REFERENCE

Steve is a professional accountant working in practice.

Kept Ltd is Steve's oldest client and as well as the usual accountancy and tax services, Steve has recently been asked to write a reference to a new landlord confirming that Kept Ltd is likely to be able to pay its rent for the next 3 years.

While this would normally not be a problem, Steve is aware that Kept Ltd has been experiencing financial difficulties over the last 6 months, so he is wary of writing such a reference. To reassure him, Kept Ltd's Chief Accountant has offered to pay Steve a large fee for supplying the reference and suggested Steve should include a disclaimer of liability.

Required:

(a)   **Analyse Steve's dilemma from an ethical point of view.**

(b)   **If Steve writes the reference, knowing Kept Ltd may not be able to pay, what crime is he potentially committing?**

(c)   **What difference would it make if Steve included a disclaimer of liability in the written reference?**

42   CYCLE

Mthbe is a professional accountant with his own small practice. He performs accountancy and tax services for a wide range of small clients including many sole traders.

Required:

(a)   **Explain, with justification, TWO areas in which Mthbe needs to keep his technical knowledge up-to-date.**

(b)   **According to the AAT CPD policy how often should Mthbe complete a CPD Cycle?**

(c)   **List the recommended stages in the AAT's CPD cycle.**

43 SARAH

Sarah is an AAT member working for a small accountancy practice.

She has received a call from a property agent asking for the following information about a client:

- Accounts for the previous three years.

- An assurance that they will be able to meet the rent for a proposed property rental.

Required:

(a) **Advise Sarah on the appropriate course of action, with regards to giving the agent the Accounts for the previous three years.**

(b) **Advise Sarah on the appropriate course of action, with regards to giving the agent an assurance the client will be able to pay.**

44 KUTCHINS

Gemma is an AAT member working for Kutchins Ltd, an engineering consultancy. She has recently started this job, having previously worked for an accountancy firm where she was the audit senior for Kirk Ltd, a competitor of Kutchins Ltd.

Required:

Explain whether Gemma is allowed to use knowledge, information and experience gained from her previous employer in her new job.

45 BEVIS

Bevis, an AAT member, has just joined a building company as a management accountant, after working for some years in a local accountancy practice.

The following situations have arisen in Bevis' first week at work.

Matter 1

When he first joined the company the Managing Director invited him out to lunch so that they could get to know each other. The Managing Director spent most of the time questioning Bevis about competitors who were clients of the firm Bevis used to work for.

Matter 2

As part of Bevis' work he needed to find out some information on behalf of the customer. When Bevis made the necessary phone call Bevis was told that the organisation did not have authority from the customer to disclose the information. When Bevis told his boss he told Bevis to ring back and pretend to be the customer.

Required:

Explain what Bevis should do in respect of the two matters above.

46 DILEMMA

Your boss has told you that there are going to be some redundancies in the company. You will not be affected, but he has named a number of people who will be, including a good friend of yours who is in the process of buying a holiday home in Cornwall. You know that your friend would not be able to afford the property if she were to lose her job and that she would pull out of the purchase if she knew about the redundancy plans.

The news of the redundancies will not be made public for several weeks.

Required:

(a) State which fundamental ethical principle is primarily involved here.

(b) Assess the ethical argument that you should tell your friend about the redundancies on the grounds it could save her unnecessary financial problems and distress.

47 JUSTIN

Justin is an AAT member in practice at Tipling LLP. He is a senior on an assurance assignment for Brittle plc.

He inherits a 10% shareholding in this client.

Required:

(a) Which type of threat does this situation represent?

(b) What would Justin's best course of action be?

48 JULIE

Julie has audited the accounts of Believe It plc as part of the assurance team for the past five years. She has been approached by Believe It plc with an offer of the Senior Accountant role.

Required:

(a) State which type of threat this situation represents.

(b) Suggest TWO safeguards the assurance firm should have in place concerning such a threat.

49 NO DEFENCE

M plc is a large UK-based building firm that specialises in public sector contracts such as schools, hospitals and sports facilities.

Having a strong green and ethical reputation is vital to M plc's chances of winning government contracts. To protect its reputation, M has an internal ethics hotline for employees to raise any concerns they might have or evidence of wrongdoing.

Due to a recent economic downturn, M plc has seen a major decline in its European business so the Board are keen to expand in other parts of the world.

Matter

In 20X9 M plc was successful in winning a major contract to build new hospitals in Country H in Africa. However, a month later, the ethics hotline received a call concerning Mr Igbinadola, the agent who represented M plc in the negotiations with the government. The call claimed that Mr Igbinadola is well known for his excessive gifts and hospitality and paid for the MP involved in the negotiations to go on a lavish holiday just weeks before the contract was awarded. The Board of M plc claims no knowledge of such gifts and is adamant it didn't authorise this.

Required:

(a)   Outline the four offences described by the UK Bribery Act 2010.

(b)   Explain the defences a commercial organisation could offer to a charge of bribery.

(c)   Discuss whether M plc could be guilty of an offence under the UK Bribery Act 2010.

50   L PLC

Andre, an AAT member, works for L plc, a UK company that exports a range of seed and other agricultural products to growers around the globe.

Recently Andre accompanied other representatives from L plc to go to a foreign country ('M') to discuss with a local farming cooperative the possible supply of a new strain of wheat that is resistant to a disease which recently swept the region.

In the meeting, the head of the cooperative told them about the problems which the relative unavailability of antiretroviral drugs cause locally in the face of a high HIV infection rate.

In a subsequent meeting with an official of M to discuss the approval of L plc's new wheat strain for import, the official suggests that L plc could pay for the necessary antiretroviral drugs and that this will be a very positive factor in the Government's consideration of the licence to import the new seed strain.

In a further meeting, the same official states that L plc should donate money to a certain charity suggested by the official which, the official assures, will then take the necessary steps to purchase and distribute the drugs.

Andre has raised concerns regarding potential bribery risks if L plc goes ahead with the suggestions made. However, the government official concerned has assured Andre that such payments comply with local laws and are standard custom and practice.

Required:

Advise the Directors of L plc, with regards to the bribery risk.

51   IN-HOUSE CODE

The directors of John Groom Ltd, a small manufacturing company, have drafted an ethical code for use within the organisation, based on ones used by competitors and the industry trade organisation. The Board also plan to encourage suppliers to adopt the code.

Required:

Explain the legal status of this code.

52 NEW CODE

Matter

Cosby plc owns a small chain of supermarkets with an emphasis on organic, local produce. The Directors of Cosby plc are concerned that, despite having better quality produce than rivals, it is not competing as well as it would like against national supermarket chains.

The Marketing Director has proposed that Cosby plc should set up a new corporate code of ethics that could be used as part of its marketing effort. He is convinced that many customers will be influenced by such a code and has suggested that the following aspects could be incorporated:

1   All products should be purchased from local farms and suppliers where appropriate.

2   All packing materials should be obtained from renewable sources where feasible.

3   All suppliers to be paid on time.

4   All suppliers to be paid fair prices as determined by the Purchasing Manager.

Required:

Comment on EACH of the ethical values suggested by the Marketing Director, highlighting the benefit of each, together with any reservations you may have concerning them.

53 PROCEDURE

Ye Lin, an AAT member in practice, works for a company that is now under investigation for corruption.

The Finance Director has told Ye Lin not to cooperate with the investigation team.

Required:

(a)   State whether Ye Lin should cooperate with the investigation or obey the FD.

(b)   State what Ye Lin could be found guilty of if she fails to cooperate with the investigation.

(c)   Describe THREE possible disciplinary actions that the AAT could apply if Ye Lin is found guilty of damaging the reputation of the association.

54 CHRIS

Chris, an AAT member, works for HJK and Co, a medium sized accountancy practice based in Manchester. Chris has performed accountancy and tax services for both Yin Ltd and Yang Ltd for many years.

Yin Ltd is currently in negotiations with the Board of Yang Ltd concerning a proposed takeover. Both Yin Ltd and Yang Ltd have requested that Chris help advise them.

Required:

(a)   State which TWO fundamental principles are threatened by the proposed takeover.

(b)   Describe the ethical conflict resolution process Chris should undertake in deciding how to act in respect of this matter. Assume that he will be able to resolve the conflict of interest without needing to seek external professional advice.

(c)   Assuming he decides he can act for one of the clients, explain TWO issues Chris must consider when carrying out his work.

55   SIMON

Simon, a member in practise, inherits from his Grandfather shares in a company that his firm audits.

Required:

(a)   **State which threat this situation represents.**

(b)   **Outline what Simon's best course of action is.**

56   LAST

Jason is an AAT member in practice. The following matter arose this week:

Matter

One evening Jason had a drink with an old friend, Brian, an AAT member currently working as an accountant for a large manufacturing company.

Brian was extremely worried about events in the company he works for. He had been asked by one of the directors to become involved in an arrangement that would lead to personal financial gain for the director at the expense of the company. Brian had been offered financial reward for this, and it had been made clear to him that he would lose his job if he didn't comply.

Required:

(a)   **State which ethical principle Brian has already breached by talking about this situation.**

(b)   **Explain what course of action is most appropriate for Brian to take immediately.**

(c)   **If the situation cannot be resolved via internal action, explain what Brian should do.**

57   SAFE AND SOUND

Lara is a professional accountant in practice. Detailed below are three matters that have arisen with respect to some of Lara's clients.

Matter A

The director of Company W, a listed company, sold a substantial shareholding prior to the announcement of worse than expected results for the company.

Matter B

Mike is CEO of Company X and is also a non-executive director of Company Y and sits on the remuneration committee of that company.

Graham is CEO of Company Y and is also a non-executive director of Company X and sits on the remuneration committee of that company.

Mike and Graham are good friends and play golf together every Saturday.

Matter C

The chairman of Company Z does not like conflict on the board.

When a new director is appointed, the chairman always ensures that the director's family members obtain highly paid jobs in the company and, in the case of children, that they are sponsored by Company Z through college.

Company Z is very profitable, although the board appears to be ineffective in querying the actions of the chairman.

Required:

For each of the situations above, identify the ethical threat to the client and recommend an ethical safeguard, explaining why that safeguard is appropriate.

58 FREE HOLIDAYS

Sarah works for a firm of accountants called B & Sons LLP and has recently introduced a new client to the firm called Leigh Davis. She has also been appointed as the audit manager for the client's company A Tours Limited which specialises in luxury holidays in the Caribbean. Leigh Davis was keen for Sarah to be appointed the audit manager for his company as he has known Sarah for a long time. He has recently offered Sarah free holidays in the Caribbean in return for her not asking questions about some irregularities in his company's financial statements.

Required:

Analyse the above scenario in relation to the law relating to bribery. In particular, explain which criminal offences the various parties have committed or are at risk of committing.

59 KEN

Ken is involved in illegal activities from which he makes a considerable amount of money.

In order to conceal his gains from the illegal activities, he bought a bookshop intending to pass off his illegally gained money as profits from the legitimate bookshop business.

Ken employs Los to act as the manager of the bookshop and Mel as his accountant to produce false business accounts for the bookshop business.

Required:

(a) **Explain what is meant by money laundering, the different categories of offence and possible punishments.**

(b) **Analyse the above scenario from the perspective of the law relating to money laundering. In particular, explain which criminal offences may have been committed by the various parties.**

60   MLRO

Jeff, a member in practice has recently come across what he believes is an investigation by the regulatory authorities into allegations of money laundering at a large client.

Required:

(a)   **Jeff decides to communicate this to the Finance Director of the client.**

State what offence Jeff will commit if he does this.

(b)   **What is the maximum sentence that Jeff can receive if found guilty of the offence.**

(c)   **Jeff's defence includes the claim that his organisation does not have a MLRO (Money Laundering Reporting Officer). In the absence of an MLRO, who should Jeff have approached with his concerns?**

(d)   **A second part of Jeff's defence is that the amount in question was only £3,000 and that this is below the de minimis limit.**

What is the de minimis limit?

61   ADAM

Adam, an AAT member within the UK, works for a firm of accountants, LOFT and Co, with a range of clients.

Matter 1

Adam has found an error in a client's tax affairs. The client has refused to disclose this known error, even after Adam has given notice of this error and an appropriate amount of time has been allowed to take action.

Required:

State to whom Adam is obliged to report this refusal to and the information surrounding it.

Matter 2

LOFT and Co recently billed a client, H Ltd, £5,000 and were very surprised when they received a cheque for £50,000 in settlement of the invoice.

The Finance Director of H Ltd explained that it was a mistake on his part but asked whether LOFT and Co could send a cheque for the overpayment of £45,000 to Q Ltd, a different company and not one of LOFT's clients.

Required:

Discuss whether or not LOFT and Co should agree to the payment.

62   DONNA

Donna, an accountant in practice, has recently been working on the tax computations for a client, Stoppard plc.

In preparing this year's tax returns Donna realised that she made an error preparing the last tax returns which resulted in an underpayment. She told the Finance Director of Stoppard plc about the error but he is refusing to tell the HMRC, claiming 'she made the mistake, not him'.

Required:

Explain what action Donna should take.

63   DUMPING

During your lunch you read an article in the FT about a case where a company was prosecuted through the courts for a breach of environmental laws regarding the dumping of toxic waste into drains, which subsequently lead to the open ocean. The case included testimony from the company's auditors which secured the prosecution.

You discussed this with one of the juniors who said that she thought that this would constitute a breach of confidentiality on behalf of the auditor.

Required:

Explain why this is not the case.

64   INTEGRITY

Frankie is an AAT member working for Lightfoots Ltd as an assistant to the management accountant. His Finance Director has asked him to post a journal to transfer £20,000, a material sum, out of maintenance costs and into non-current assets, thus boosting profit for the period. Frankie has checked the details and feels that there is no justification for the journal.

Required:

Explain what action Frankie should take, highlighting both internal and external courses of action.

65   BENEFITS

Jacqui has recently been appointed as the chief accountant for a small public sector organisation. The other members of the senior management team (SMT) are very pleased with her appointment as they have really struggled to attract, recruit and retain good staff.

At the last meeting of the SMT it was decided that the benefits package for senior staff (including the SMT) was inadequate and that it needed revising.

Jacqui was asked to draw up the new package and, after considerable research and benchmarking, has decided that a significant increase is needed in the benefits package.

Required:

(a) Discuss which ethical principles are potentially compromised here.

(b) Identify which factors Jacqui should consider before making a decision what to do.

(c) Explain what the best course of action would be.

66 SUSHIL

Sushil is a member in business. His manager has asked him to falsify the accounts and has made it clear that if he refuses then he will lose his job.

Required:

(a) State which type of threat this situation represents.

(b) Explain what the best course of action would be.

67 TRUE

Naill is an AAT member working for a large building company. The finance director has asked him to adjust some of the sales figures, so that the year-end final numbers look better than they actually are.

Required:

(a) Discuss whether Naill should do as the Finance Director instructs?

(b) Explain what is mean by 'false accounting'.

68 MEERA

Meera works for a large accountancy firm as a tax specialist. Recently two matters have arisen:

Matter 1

On Monday Meera was in a meeting with a potential new client.

The potential client started by stating that he felt Meera's fees proposal was far too high and she needed to reduce them substantially.

He then said that he believed his tax bill for the previous year was also too high but if Meera guaranteed to reduce his tax bill, then he would come to her firm.

Meera had a quick look at the figures and she believed the sum looked reasonable.

(a) Explain what Meera should do in response to the client's requests.

Matter 2

On Tuesday Meera had a dispute with Greg, a new client. After analysing Greg's tax affairs Meera had found a material error in the previous year's tax return that resulted in an underpayment of tax. The previous tax computations were prepared by Greg's previous accountant.

Meera advised Greg to tell HMRC about the error but so far he has refused to do so, claiming it is 'their problem, not his'.

(b)   **Should Meera tell HRMC about the error?**

(c)   **What should Meera do if Greg continues to refuse to inform the HMRC?**

69   DISMISS

Sarah, a member employed in a division of a large building company, believes that one of the contract managers is attempting to short-cut building regulations by using substandard building materials in a new school.

Sarah has spoken to an internal whistle-blowing helpline about the situation and now the divisional manager is threatening to have her dismissed 'for not being a team player'.

Explain whether or not Sarah is protected by the PIDA (1998)?

70   SUSTENANCE

At a recent Board meeting of Sustenance plc the topic of sustainability arose. The main view given was that attempts to incorporate sustainability would inevitably increase costs and reduce profits. When the Finance Director tried to explain that this was not the case, the Marketing Director commented that sustainability was nothing to do with accountants anyway.

Required:

(a)   **Outline the roles of professional accountants in contributing to sustainability.**

(b)   **Describe three ways in which an increased emphasis on sustainability can result in improved profits for a firm.**

71   HOGGS FURNITURE

Jacob is a professional accountant working for Hoggs Furniture Ltd ('Hoggs'), a furniture manufacturer that supplies many high street retailers.

Matter

At the last management meeting it was announced that a major client of the company was threatening to terminate their contract with Hoggs unless it could demonstrate a clear commitment to sustainability.

The team were unclear what this meant for Hoggs and asked Jacob to investigate further.

Required:

(a)   **Explain what is meant by 'sustainability'.**

(b)   **Explain FOUR areas that Jacob should appraise in order to answer the client's concerns.**

(c)   **List THREE other ways Jacob can contribute to sustainability through his role as an accountant.**

72   MLC

MLC is a clothing retailer who imports clothes from diverse suppliers worldwide. MLC has a very strong, well-publicised corporate ethical code.

The company accountant has just found out that one of MLC suppliers use child labour in the manufacture of their clothes and pay very low wages with cramped, dangerous conditions. This is in breach of contract conditions with that supplier.

This was raised at the last Board meeting and a wide range of opinions were discussed, including the following:

- "Place more orders with the supplier – it's cheap labour so the margins are good, which should keep the shareholders happy."

- "Leave things as they are and hope the information doesn't get out."

- "Continue trading with the supplier but investigate the claims quietly."

- "Cancel all contracts with the supplier and release a press statement stating how the company will always act quickly and decisively if unethical practices are suspected."

Advise the board.

73   STEPHANIE

Stephanie has worked in the finance department of Alpha for 5 years and has been promoted to work alongside the management accountant. Stephanie is currently working towards an AAT qualification.

The AAT-qualified management accountant of Alpha has told Stephanie that he works closely with department heads to produce their annual budgets. He is happy to allow significant 'slack' to be built in to these budgets to make them easier to achieve since, in his view, this makes Alpha a much more relaxed place to work.

Following this conversation, Stephanie overheard the management accountant agreeing to alter budgeted production figures to make them easier to achieve in return for tickets to a major football game. When she questioned her boss, he told her no harm was done since the budgeted figures are subjective anyway.

Discuss which ethical principles the management accountant is in breach of?

74   STEVEN

As financial controller Steven has been asked to sign off N&Q Ltd's year-end accounts. He joined the company only three months ago.

The accounts include a note that is incorrect. Having investigated the matter, Steven recognises that this is a genuine mistake and not a deliberate attempt to mislead.

The Managing Director does not want to produce new accounts because of its inherent cost, but Steven does not feel it appropriate that he signs off something that has an error in it.

What action should Steven take?

75 INTEGRITY

Frankie is an AAT member working for Lightfoots Ltd as an assistant to the management accountant. His finance director has asked him to post a journal to transfer £20,000, a material sum, out of maintenance costs and into non-current assets, thus boosting profit for the period. Frankie has checked the details and feels that there is no justification for the journal.

Required:

Explain what Frankie should do, highlighting both internal and external courses of action.

76 FINANCE

'Ultimate DPF' is a sole trader who makes exhaust systems for diesel-powered cars. Jenny Green, the owner and founder of the business, is looking at expanding operations and is considering different ways of raising the additional finance required.

Option 1

The first approach Jenny is considering is finding new business partners to come into the business with her but is unsure about whether to set up the business as a partnership or a limited company.

Explain to Jenny THREE differences between partnerships and limited companies (excluding those relating to raising finance) and TWO implications this choice will make on raising the finance required.

Difference 1
Difference 2
Difference 3
Implication for finance 1
Implication for finance 2

Option 2

The second approach Jenny is considering is to try to raise a bank loan and read online that banks like to look at the Statement of Financial Position (SOFP) when assessing a loan application. This confused Jenny as she thought the SOFP was produced primarily for shareholders.

Explain THREE elements of a SOFP that a bank would be interested in and why

Aspect of SOFP	Reason why the bank would look at this
1	
2	
3	

List THREE stakeholders (other than a bank) who would use a SOFP and explain why

Stakeholder	Reason why they would use the SOFP
1	
2	
3	

77 ACCOUNTING FUNDAMENTALS

1 Describe and explain what the accounting equation is, its importance and how it is used.

2 Describe and explain what the Statement of Profit and Loss is, its importance and how it is used.

3 Describe and explain what the Statement of Financial Position is, its importance and how it is used.

4 Compare the Statement of Profit and Loss and the Statement of Financial position by explaining the similarities/differences between the two, and the advantages and disadvantages of each.

78 CASH

Explain THREE reasons why the net profit of a business for a period is not necessarily the same as the net cash generated in the same period. Give TWO examples for each reason.

Reason 1
Reason 2
Reason 3

TASK 5 COMPUTER ASSESSED

Assessment objective 5	Analyse, interpret and report management accounting data

79 ORGANISATION

An organisation has three departments Mending, Stores and Canteen. The budgeted overhead costs for the organisation are as follows:

	£
Rent	30,000
Building maintenance costs	45,000
Machinery insurance	2,400
Machinery depreciation	11,000
Machinery running cost	6,000
Power	7,000

The following information about the various cost centres is also available:

	Mending	Stores	Canteen	Total
Floor space (m²)	8,000	5,000	2,000	15,000
Power usage %	80	10	10	100
Value of machinery (£000)	140	110	–	250
Machinery hours (000)	50	30	–	80
Value of equipment (£000)	15	5	–	20
Specific costs £	4,000	1,000	2,000	7,000

Complete the overhead apportionment of the costs to the three departments.

Overhead cost	Basis	Mending £	Stores £	Canteen £	Total £
Specific overheads	Allocate	4,000	1,000	2,000	7,000
Rent	*choose from the options below				
Building maintenance	Floor space	24,000	15,000	6,000	45,000
Machinery insurance	Value of machinery	1,344	1,056	0	2,400
Machinery depreciation	*choose from the options below				
Machinery running cost	Machinery hours	3,750	2,250	0	6,000
Power	*choose from the options below				
Total					

Options:

Floor space (m²)
Power usage %
Value of machinery (£000)
Machinery hours (000)
Value of equipment (£000)

80 ORGANISATION PART 2

An organisation has three departments Mending, Stores and Canteen.

The budgeted overhead allocated and apportioned into each department are as follows:

	£
Mending	60,854
Stores	34,846
Canteen	12,700

The following information about the various cost centres is also available:

	Mending	Stores	Canteen
Number of employees	15	5	2
Value of stores requisitions (£000)	50	–	–

Reapportion the costs to the production department. Use minus signs where appropriate.

Overhead cost	Basis	Mending £	Stores £	Canteen £	Total £
Sub-Total		60,854	34,846	12,700	108,400
Re-apportion Canteen	*choose from the options below				
Re-apportion Stores	*choose from the options below				
Total					

Options:

Number of employees
Value of stores requisitions (£000)

81   PACKAGING

Packaging Ltd has the following original budget and actual performance for product RB for the year ending 31 July.

Complete the table below to show a flexed budget and the resulting variances against this budget for the year. Round to the nearest £1,000. Adverse variance must be denoted with a minus sign

	Original Budget	Flexed Budget	Actual	Variance
Volume sold	180,000		259,200	
	£000	£000	£000	£000
Sales revenue	3,600		6,480	
Less costs:				
Direct materials	630		954	
Direct labour	720		864	
Fixed overheads	1,764		2,210	
Operating profit	486		2,452	

82   LF LTD

LF Ltd manufactures three products – X, Y and Z – that use the same machines.

The budgeted statements of profit or loss for the three products are as follows:

	X	Y	Z
	£000	£000	£000
Sales	1,000	1,125	625
Prime costs	(500)	(562.50)	(437.50)
Variable overheads	(250)	(187.50)	(62.50)
Fixed overheads	(200)	(315)	(130)
Profit/(loss)	50	60	(5)
Annual sales demand (units)	5,000	7,500	2,500
Machine hours per unit	20	21	26

Fixed overheads are absorbed on the basis of machine hours. The budgeted machine hours based on normal capacity were 322,500 hours.

However, after the budget had been formulated, an unforeseen condition has meant that during the next period the available machine capacity has been limited to 296,500 hours.

Task 1

Determine the order of priority (rankings) of production of the three products.

	X	Y	Z
Contribution per unit (£)			
Machine hours per unit (hours)			
Contribution per machine hour (£)			
Rank			

Task 2

Determine the optimum production plan for the next period and the resulting profit.

Product	Units	Contribution per unit	Total contribution £
X/Y/Z			
X/Y/Z			
X/Y/Z			
Total Contribution			
Less: Fixed costs			
Profit			

83 HEATH

Heath Ltd makes product 'H' which has a selling price of £19 per unit with a total variable cost of £12 per unit. Heath Ltd estimates that the fixed costs associated with this product are £17,150.

(a) **Calculate the budgeted breakeven, in units, for product H.**

units

(b) **Calculate the budgeted breakeven, in £s, for product H.**

£

(c) **Complete the table below to show the budgeted margin of safety in units and the margin of safety percentage if Heath Ltd sells 4,000 units or 5,000 units of product H.**

Units of H sold	4,000	5,000
Margin of safety (units)		
Margin of safety percentage (2dp)		

(d) **If Heath Ltd wishes to make a profit of £24,850, how many units of H must it sell?**

units

(e)   If Heath Ltd increases the selling price of H by £2 what will be the impact on the breakeven point and the margin of safety assuming no change in the number of units sold?

A   The breakeven point will decrease and the margin of safety will stay the same

B   The breakeven point will decrease and the margin of safety will increase

C   The breakeven point will stay the same but the margin of safety will decrease

D   The breakeven point will increase and the margin of safety will decrease

84   BLINDS

One of the machines in the Finishing department is nearing the end of its useful life and Blinds Ltd is considering purchasing a replacement machine.

Estimates have been made for the initial capital cost, sales income and operating costs of the replacement machine, which is expected to have a useful life of three years:

	Year 0 £000	Year 1 £000	Year 2 £000	Year 3 £000
Capital expenditure	547			
Other cash flows:				
Sales income		290	340	400
Operating costs		120	120	120

The company appraises capital investment projects using a 10% cost of capital.

(a)   Complete the table below and calculate the net present value of the proposed replacement machine (to the nearest £000).

	Year 0 £000	Year 1 £000	Year 2 £000	Year 3 £000
Capital expenditure				
Sales income				
Operating costs				
Net cash flows				
PV factors	1.000	0.909	0.826	0.751
Discounted cash flows				
Net present value				

(b)   Calculate the payback period.

(c)   Estimate the IRR of this project

A   0%

B   5%

C   10%

D   15%

(d) **If the NPV of a project is nil then the cost of capital equals the Internal Rate of Return (IRR)** True or false?

(e) **If the IRR of an investment is higher than the company's cost of capital then the investment should go ahead.** True or false?

85 FIFO AVCO

Which method of inventory valuation is being described?

Characteristic	FIFO	AVCO
Potentially out of date valuation on issues.		
The valuation of inventory rarely reflects the actual purchase price of the material.		
This inventory valuation method is particularly suited to inventory that consist of liquid materials e.g. oil.		
This inventory valuation method is particularly suited to inventory that has a short shelf life e.g. dairy products.		
In times of rising prices this method will give higher profits.		
In times of rising prices this method will give lower profits.		
Inventory is valued at the average of the cost of purchases.		
Inventory is valued at the most recent purchase cost.		

86 DIRECT INDIRECT

How would the following labour costs be classified?

Cost	Direct	Indirect
Basic pay for production workers		
Supervisors wages		
Bonus for salesman		
Production workers overtime premium due to general pressures		
Holiday pay for production workers		
Sick pay for supervisors		
Time spent by production workers cleaning the machinery		

87 BONUS

A company employs a group of production workers who, as well as earning basic pay, are also paid a weekly group bonus based on their productivity during each week.

The group has a standard output of 200 units of production per hour worked. All output in excess of this level earns a bonus for each of the employees.

The bonus % is calculated as:

$$10\% \times \frac{\text{Excess production (units)}}{\text{Standard production (units)}} \times 100$$

The bonus rate per hour is then calculated as: bonus % × £20.

The following information relates to this group's performance last week:

	Hours worked	Actual production (units)
Monday	900	235,000
Tuesday	850	222,500
Wednesday	900	232,500
Thursday	910	240,000
Friday	870	247,500
Saturday	400	172,500
Total	4,830	1,350,000

(a) Use the table below to calculate the group bonus rate per hour and the total bonus to be paid to the group.

	Units
Actual production	
Less standard production (based on actual hours worked)	
Excess production	
Bonus % (nearest whole %)	
Group bonus rate per hour £ (2 decimal places)	
Total group bonus £ (nearest whole £)	

(b) An employee in this group worked for 40 hours last week, and is paid a basic rate of £9.30 per hour. The employee's total pay for last week was:

£

88   HOLDINGS LTD

The coating department of JH Holdings Ltd uses process costing for coating metal components with a hard layer of titanium nitride to increase longevity.

The process account for January for one particular process has been partly completed but the following information is also relevant:

Four employees worked on this process during January. Each employee worked 30 hours per week for 4 weeks and was paid £12 per hour.

Overheads are absorbed on the basis of £8 per labour hour.

JH Holdings Ltd expects a normal loss of 10% during this process, which it then sells for scrap at £5 per kg.

Complete the process account below for January.

Description	Units	Unit cost £	Total cost £	Description	Units	Unit cost £	Total cost £
Input – components	300	11.25	3,375	Normal loss		5.00	
Materials – coating			500	Output	290		
Labour							
Overheads							

89   SILVER

Silver makes key rings on a production line. Details of the process in period 2 are as follows:

OWIP   250 units

Costs incurred so far

        Materials   £53,800

        Conversion   £42,000

Degrees of completion

        Materials   100%

        Conversion   60%

Completed output   3,200 units

Costs incurred in Period 2:

        Materials   £135,000

        Conversion   £98,800

Calculate the cost per equivalent unit using the AVCO method of valuing WIP.

Equivalent units	Material	Conversion
Cost per EU		

90 DEBIT OR CREDIT?

(a) What would be the double entry for an issue of indirect production materials?

A	Dr Materials control account	Cr Finished goods control account
B	Dr Production overhead control a/c	Cr Materials control account
C	Dr Work-in-progress control account	Cr Production overhead control a/c
D	Dr Work-in-progress control account	Cr Materials control account

(b) How would the cost be recorded in the cost ledger if the direct labour costs in a manufacturing company are £95,000?

A	Debit Work-in-progress £95,000,	Credit Labour £95,000
B	Debit Labour £95,000,	Credit Bank £95,000
C	Debit Labour £95,000,	Credit Work-in-progress £95,000
D	Debit Bank £95,000,	Credit Labour £95,000

(c) What would the accounting entries be for £10,000 of over-absorbed overheads?

A	Dr Work-in-progress control account	Cr Overhead control account
B	Dr Statement of profit or loss	Cr Work-in-progress control account
C	Dr Statement of profit or loss	Cr Overhead control account
D	Dr Overhead control account	Cr Statement of profit or loss

91 ANIMAL BEDDING

Animal Bedding Ltd has prepared a forecast for the next quarter for the production and sales of its product 'Dreamy Bedding'.

Animal Bedding Ltd budgets to produce 900 animal beds and sell 500 of them. The cost and revenue for this budget is as follows:

	£000
Sales	25,000
Direct materials	3,780
Direct labour	8,820
Fixed production overheads	1,800
Advertising (fixed cost)	1,005

Animal Bedding Ltd has no opening inventory of the Dreamy Bedding.

Produce a marginal costing statement of profit or loss and an absorption costing statement of profit or loss:

Marginal costing	£000	£000
Sales		
Opening inventory		
Production costs		
Less: Closing inventory		
Less: Cost of sales		
Contribution		
Less: Fixed costs		
Profit for the period		

Absorption costing	£000	£000
Sales		
Opening inventory		
Production costs		
Less: Closing inventory		
Less: Cost of sales		
Gross profit		
Less: Non-production cost		
Profit for the period		

92 OAR

(a) A cost centre has an overhead absorption rate of £4.25 per machine hour, based on a budgeted activity level of 12,400 machine hours.

In the period covered by the budget, actual machine hours worked were 2% more than the budgeted hours and the actual overhead expenditure incurred in the cost centre was £56,389.

What was the total over or under absorption of overheads in the cost centre for the period?

A   £1,054 over absorbed

B   £2,635 under absorbed

C   £3,689 over absorbed

D   £3,689 under absorbed

(b)   A law firm recovers overheads on chargeable consulting hours. Budgeted overheads were £615,000 and actual consulting hours were 32,150. Overheads were under-recovered by £35,000. Actual overheads were £694,075.

What is the budgeted overhead absorption rate per hour (to 2 decimal places)?

A   £20.21

B   £20.50

C   £21.59

D   £22.68

(c)   A firm absorbs overheads on labour hours. In one period 11,500 hours were worked, actual overheads were £138,000 and there was £23,000 over-absorption.

What was the overhead absorption rate per hour (to 2 decimal places)?

£ [   ]

TASK 6 HUMAN ASSESSED

Assessment objective 6	Prepare financial accounting information, comprising extended trial balances and final accounts for sole traders and partnerships

Note: This task in the assessment is human marked. Students will be required to make both text and numeric entries.

93   HIGHLAND

You work for Highland, a business that makes and sells parts for vintage cars. You have been provided with an ETB that has been started by the current bookkeeper. However, she is now on holiday and the owner of Highland has asked that you create the adjustments and enter them onto the ETB to save time.

Make the appropriate entries in the adjustments column of the extended trial balance to take account of the following. The year-end date is 31 December 20X5.

(a)   The allowances for doubtful debts figure is to be adjusted to 2% of receivables.

(b)   A credit note received from a supplier for goods returned was mislaid. It has since been found and has not yet been accounted for. It was for £2,000 net plus £400 VAT.

(c)   Rent is payable yearly in advance. For the 12 months to 31/10/X5 the rent is £12,000, the prepayment bought down has been included in the ledger balance. For the 12 months to 31/10/X6 the rent is £15,000.

(d)   Inventory is valued at cost at £14,890. However, there was a leak in the storage cupboard and £3,000 worth of items has been damaged and need to be written off.

(e)   The electricity bill of £450 for the 3 months ended 31 January 20X6 was received and paid in February 20X6.

Extended trial balance

Ledger account	Ledger balances		Adjustments	
	Dr £	**Cr** £	**Dr** £	**Cr** £
Accruals		1,330		
Advertising	1,800			
Bank	17,912			
Capital		40,000		
Closing inventory				
Depreciation charge				
Drawings	14,700			
Fixtures and fittings – accumulated depreciation		945		
Fixtures and fittings – cost	6,099			
Irrecoverable debts	345			
Allowance for doubtful debt adjustment				
Electricity	1,587			
Loan		10,000		

Opening inventory	5,215	
Prepayment		
Allowance for doubtful debts		485
Purchases	78,921	
Purchase returns		
PLCA		14,000
Rent	25,000	
Revenue		145,825
SLCA	9,500	
VAT control account		11,453
Wages	62,959	
	224,038	224,038

94 ETB

You have the following extended trial balance. The adjustments have already been correctly entered. You now need to extend the figures into the statement of profit or loss and statement of financial position columns. Make the columns balance by entering figures and a label in the partner correct places.

Extended trial balance

Ledger account	Ledger balances		Adjustments		Statement of profit or loss		Statement of financial position	
	Dr £	Cr £	Dr £	Cr £	Dr £	Cr £	Dr £	Cr £
Accruals		2,300		425				
Advertising	1,800							
Bank	7,912		1,175					
Capital		40,000						
Closing inventory			6,590	6,590				
Depreciation charge			821					
Drawings	14,700							
Fixtures and fittings – accumulated depreciation		945		821				
Fixtures and fittings – cost	6,099							
Interest	345							
Light and heat	1,587		706					
Loan		10,000						
Opening inventory	5,215							
Prepayments	485		927	281				

Purchases	75,921									
PLCA		14,000								
Rent and rates	38,000			927						
Revenue		145,825								
SLCA	9,500			1,175						
VAT control account		11,453								
Wages	62,959									
	224,523	224,523	10,219	10,219						

95 VINCENT

You have the following trial balance for a sole trader known as Vincent Trading. All the necessary year-end adjustments have been made.

Vincent Trading has a policy of showing trade receivables net of any allowance for doubtful debts and showing trade payables and sundry payables as one total figure.

The statement of profit or loss for Vincent Trading shows a profit of £8,810 for the period.

Prepare a statement of financial position for the business for the year ended 30 June 20X8.

Vincent Trading Trial balance as at 30 June 20X8	Dr £	Cr £
Accruals		750
Bank		1,250
Capital		17,000
Closing inventory	7,850	7,850
Discounts received		900
Sundry payables		1,450
Purchase ledger control account		6,800
Depreciation charge	1,600	
Discounts allowed	345	
Allowance for doubtful debts adjustment	295	
Equipment accumulated depreciation		4,500
Wages	24,000	
Sales ledger control account	7,800	
Rent	5,250	
Revenue		164,000
Disposal		450
Prepayments	3,200	
Purchases	125,000	

Sales returns	1,500	
Opening inventory	3,450	
Equipment at cost	17,500	
Drawings	8,000	
General expenses	2,950	
Allowance for doubtful debts		840
VAT		2,950
	208,740	208,740

Vincent Trading

Statement of financial position as at 30 June 20X8

	£	£	£
Non-current assets	**Cost**	**Depreciation**	**Carrying amount**
Current assets			
Current liabilities			
Net current assets			
Net assets			
Financed by:			
Opening capital			
Add:			
Less:			
Closing capital			

96 BEALE

You are preparing the statement of financial position for Beale, a sole trader. All the necessary year-end adjustments have been made.

Beale has a policy of showing trade receivables net of any allowance for doubtful debts. The statement of profit or loss for Beale shows a loss of £4,350 for the period.

Prepare a statement of financial position for the business for the year ended 30 June 20X6.

Beale – Trial balance as at 30 June 20X6		
	Dr £	Cr £
Accruals		3,150
Administration expenses	45,000	
Bank		2,250
Capital		85,000
Cash	500	
Closing inventory	17,500	17,500
Depreciation charge	9,000	
Disposal of non-current asset		1,500
Motor vehicles at cost	45,000	
Motor vehicles accumulated depreciation		20,000
Opening inventory	15,000	
Allowance for doubtful debts		1,450
Allowance for doubtful debts adjustment	200	
Purchases	75,000	
Purchases ledger control account		23,750
Revenue		130,000
Sales ledger control account	68,550	
Selling expenses	9,150	
Drawings	3,200	
VAT		3,500
Total	288,100	288,100

Beale – Statement of financial position as at 30 June 20X6			
	£	£	£
Non-current assets	Cost	Depreciation	Carrying amount
Current assets			
Current liabilities			
Net current assets			
Net assets			
Financed by:			
Opening capital			
Less:			
Less:			
Closing capital			

97   PEG

You have the following information about a partnership business:

The financial year ends on 30 June.

- The partners are Gertrude, Eddie and Polonius.

- Partners' annual salaries

    - Gertrude   £18,000

    - Eddie   nil

    - Polonius   £36,000

- Partners' interest on capital

    - Gertrude   £2,000 per annum

    - Eddie   £2,000 per annum

    - Polonius   £2,000 per annum

- Partners' sales commission earned during the year

  - Gertrude   £8,250

  - Eddie   £6,800

  - Polonius   £4,715

- Profit share

  - Gertrude   40%

  - Eddie   40%

  - Polonius   20%

The statement of profit or loss for the partnership shows a profit for the year ended 30 June 20X9 of £220,000 before appropriations.

Prepare the appropriation account for the partnership for the year ended 30 June 20X9. Enter zeros where appropriate and use minus signs for deductions.

Partnership appropriation account for the year ended 30 June 20X9

	£
Profit for the year	
Salaries:	
Gertrude	
Eddie	
Polonius	
Interest on capital:	
Gertrude	
Eddie	
Polonius	
Sales commission:	
Gertrude	
Eddie	
Polonius	
Profit available for distribution	

Profit share:	
Gertrude	
Eddie	
Polonius	
Total residual profit distributed	

98   CG

You have the following information about a partnership:

- The partners are Cordelia and Goneril, and the partnership produces luxury gifts for Fathers' Day and other special occasions.

- Regan joined the partnership on 1 May 20X7 when she introduced £128,000 into the business bank account.

- Profit share, effective until 30 April 20X7

    - Cordelia   35%

    - Goneril   65%

- Profit share, effective from 1 May 20X7

    - Cordelia   25%

    - Goneril   45%

    - Regan   30%

- Goodwill was valued at £105,000 on 30 April 20X7.

- Goodwill is to be introduced into the partners' capital accounts on 30 April and then eliminated on 1 May.

(a)   Show the entries required to introduce the goodwill into the partnership accounting records.

Account name	Dr	Cr

Cordelia is thinking of leaving the partnership next year. It is estimated that Regan's good reputation will have added £22,000 to the goodwill value by then.

(b)   Calculate the goodwill to be introduced into Cordelia's capital account at the time of her departure.

£_____

99   SHAKE A SPEAR

Macbeth, Hamlet and Will are in partnership selling cases for mobile phones.

- Will retired from the partnership on 30 June 20X5. He has agreed that the partnership will pay what he is due from the bank account in full.

- Profit share, effective until 30 June 20X5

    - Macbeth   30%

    - Hamlet   40%

    - Will   30%

- Profit share, effective from 1 July 20X5

  - Macbeth   50%

  - Hamlet   50%

- Goodwill was valued at £50,000 on 30 June 20X5.

- Goodwill is to be introduced into the partners' capital accounts on 30 June and then eliminated on 1 July.

- At the 30 June 20X5 the partners had the following balances on their capital and current accounts:

  - Macbeth   £7,000 (capital a/c) and £11,000 (current a/c)

  - Hamlet   £8,000 (capital a/c) and £9,000 (current a/c)

  - Will   £9,000 (capital a/c) and £7,000 (current a/c)

Prepare the capital account for Will, showing clearly the transfer from the current account and the amount paid to Will on his retirement.

Capital account – Will

		Balance b/d	9,000

100   LEAF AND PETAL

Leaf and Petal are in partnership manufacturing and selling rustic wooden furniture. The business was set up two years ago when Leaf invested £10,000 capital, and Petal £15,000. No further capital has been injected since. In the year ended 31 December 20X5 they made a profit of £67,000. Their partnership agreement states the following:

Interest on capital to be provided at 6% per annum:

Leaf   £600

Petal   £900

Leaf to be allocated a salary of £12,000

Leaf drew £5,000 from the business on 1 January 20X5 and another £7,000 on 1 July 20X5. Petal drew £10,000 on 1 July 20X5.

Interest to be charged on drawings at a rate of 3% per annum:

Leaf   £255

Petal   £150

Balance of profits to be shared in the ratio 3:2.

At the start of the year the balances on the current accounts were:

Leaf   £7,700 Cr

Petal   £3,200 Dr

Show how this information is presented in the partners' current and capital accounts.

Capital Account

	Leaf	Petal		Leaf	Petal
	£	£		£	£

Current Account

	Leaf	Petal		Leaf	Petal
	£	£		£	£

Section 2

ANSWERS TO PRACTICE QUESTIONS

TASK 1 COMPUTER ASSESSED

1 CODE OF ETHICS

	True	False
An accountant is under no duty to disclose the limitations of their expertise to the client		✓ (130.6)
An accountant is only responsible for his or her own professional qualifications and training		✓ (130.5)
An accountant may need to compromise the most precise attention to detail in preparing work in order to meet a reasonable deadline	✓ (130.4)	

130.6 of the Code of Ethics states that 'where appropriate, a professional accountant should make clients, employers or other users of the professional services aware of limitations inherent in the services to avoid the misinterpretation of an expression of opinion as an assertion of fact'.

130.5 of the Code of Ethics states that 'a professional accountant should take steps to ensure that those working under the professional accountant's authority in a professional capacity have appropriate training and supervision'.

130.4 of the Code of Ethics state that 'diligence encompasses the responsibility to act in accordance with the requirements of an assignment, carefully, thoroughly and on a timely basis'. Inevitably, diligence represents a balance between punctiliousness and punctuality!

2 INTEGRITY

All of these are potentially breaches of the principle of integrity. Even if information is freely available, it may not be clear that it is important in the context of the work undertaken. As such, the accountant may be misleading the client by leaving it to the client to find out something. Similarly, partial information may be highly misleading. Forgetting to mention important information, unless inadvertent, could be classed as being reckless. There is a duty to be careful that is bound up with the concept of integrity. Regardless of the duty of trust and confidence, the client should not be kept in the dark to avoid embarrassment. It may be in the latter circumstances, that some urgent consultations within the firm or with a regulator or legal advisers may be appropriate.

3   CONFIDENTIAL

B is correct. Although a client might request the disclosure of information, there may be certain circumstances when that information might include other confidential information, relating to another party. However, when refusing to disclose, reasons should be given and a second opinion in principle might be sought from the person responsible for Information and Data compliance in your organisations. Requests from the regulator, unless they are acting unlawfully, will normally be appropriate to disclose information.

Requests made by solicitors, are not in themselves, requests where there is a legal obligation to disclose. The reason for the request should be a reason where there is a legal or professional obligation to disclose or where the person requesting the information through the solicitor is the sole subject of it. Solicitors' letters should be dealt with in a courteous and timely way, but should not be assumed to have any greater weight in themselves than a request by any other member of the public.

Requests by your employer, other than as part of regulatory review or because the matter is being dealt with by a variety of people across the office, all subject to the same confidentiality, should be treated with care and should fall in the category of acceptable disclosures within the terms of your Data and Information Management procedures. Most damaging breaches of confidentiality occur as a result of internal disclosure where the recipient is unaware of the confidential nature of the material they are receiving.

4   THREATS

Self-interest threats	Preparing accounts for a campaign group of which the accountant is a leading member
Self-review threats	Preparing accounts under an unrealistically imposed deadline by a major client
Advocacy threats	Preparing accounts for your close relative's business
Familiarity threats	Preparing accounts for your spouse's business
Intimidation threats	Preparing accounts and providing a basic audit function on those accounts

Self-interest – Preparing accounts for your spouse's business will clearly cause a personal conflict of interests.

Self-review – In this situation the accountant would be reviewing, as auditor, the work that they had themselves completed which would hinder their independence.

Advocacy – Being a member of the campaign group, the accountant will be seen to be advocating the group.

Familiarity – Preparing accounts for someone that you are very familiar with can put pressure on the accountant to act favourably towards, in this situation, their relative.

Intimidation – Not wanting to lose their major client, the accountant may feel intimidated into meeting the deadline at the cost of the accuracy of their work.

5   E

D is the correct answer

E stands to make a gain if the figures are manipulated to get a better bonus, hence E is in a position of a self-interest threat.

6   R

C is the correct answer

7   CX

(a)   A and D

According to the Code of ethics CX is in a position where integrity and objectivity may be compromising.

Integrity – This principle imposes an obligation to be truthful and honest on the accountant. A professional accountant should not be associated with reports or other information where she/he believes that the information contains misleading statements. This seems to be the case with the revised forecasts; CX believes that the revised forecasts are 'grossly overstated'.

Objectivity – A professional accountant should not allow conflict of interest or undue influence of others to override professional or business judgements or to compromise their professional judgements. The management board are overriding CX's professional and business judgement as they are imposing their assumptions on the forecast profits.

(b)

	Dealing with an ethical dilemma
1	Gather evidence and document the problem
2	Report internally to immediate management
3	Report internally to higher management
4	Report externally
5	Remove herself from the situation

8   PRINCIPLES

Principle	Interpretation
Professional competence and due care	Maintaining a relevant level of professional knowledge and skills so that a competent service can be provided.
Professional behaviour	Complying with relevant laws and regulations.
Integrity	Being straightforward, honest and truthful in all professional and business relationships.
Confidentiality	Not disclosing information unless there is specific permission or a legal or professional duty to do so.
Objectivity	Not allowing bias, conflict of interest or the influence of other people to override professional judgement.

9   ACTION

C is the correct answer

The basic principle here is that of confidentiality. To go outside of the business and professional environment in this manner without first considering the other options presented would not be following recommended process.

A – AAT's ethics helpline exists to give members advice and is not a breach of confidentiality as it is within the professional arena. B – Reporting the company to the environment agency would comply with relevant legislation, however you would need to sure of your facts before whistle blowing. D – The Audit committee should be all NEDs and therefore a logical place to go, particularly as they are also responsible for the whistle blowing policy.

10   FUNDAMENTAL PRINCIPLES

Confidentiality	✔
Honesty	
Objectivity	✔
Respect	
Integrity	✔

11   ETHICS AND LAW

If a person complies with the letter of the law she will always be acting ethically.	
Ethics in business is the application of ethical values to business.	✔
If a company has a code of ethics this will eliminate the need for legislation.	

The law must always be obeyed but just obeying the law does not necessarily mean those actions are ethical. As a consequence of unethical behaviour the public could lose trust in the accounting profession but simply having a code of ethics will not eliminate the need for legislation; the code must be followed.

12   ISSUES

A is the correct answer

B, C and D options are examples of good governance rather than an ethical issue.

13   BREACHES

You have been told that one of your colleagues in the accounts department has regularly submitted inflated expenses claims. This is a breach of the fundamental principle of objectivity.	
You are aware that a colleague in the accounts department regularly takes home reports to check and does so after a few cocktails. This is a breach of the fundamental principle of professional behaviour.	
You are employed as Management Accountant and have been asked to dismiss one of your colleagues for misconduct. You are aware that this is untrue and that the Company is trying to reduce the workforce without making the due redundancy payments. This is a breach of the fundamental principle of integrity.	✓

Option (1) is a breach of the fundamental principle of professional behaviour and option (2) is a breach of professional competence and due care.

TASK 2 COMPUTER ASSESSED

14   PIXIE PAPERS

Has the correct net price been calculated?	Y
Has the total invoice price been calculated correctly?	N
What would be the VAT amount charged if the invoice was correct?	£100.00
What would be the total amount charged if the invoice was correct?	£600.00

15   PAINTS R US

Has the correct net price been calculated?	Y
Has the total invoice price been calculated correctly?	Y
What would be the VAT amount charged if the invoice was correct?	£32.00
What would be the total amount charged if the invoice was correct?	£192.00

16   MONT

Sales account

	£		£
		Bank	2,200
		Receivables (3,840 × 100/120)	3,200

Bank account

	£		£
Sales/VAT (sales tax)	2,640	Purchases/VAT (sales tax)	1,680

Receivables account

	£		£
Sales/VAT (sales tax)	3,840		

VAT (sales tax) account

	£		£
Payables (1,800 × 20/120)	300	Bank	440
Bank (1,400 × 20%)	280	Receivables (3,840 × 20/120)	640
Balance c/d	500		
	1,080		1,080
		Balance b/d	500

Purchases account

	£		£
Payables (1,800 × 100/120)	1,500		
Bank	1,400		

Payables account

	£		£
		Purchases/VAT (sales tax)	1,800

The credit balance remaining on the VAT (sales tax) account is the amount of VAT (sales tax) owed to the tax authorities (HM Revenue and Customs).

17   BESS

Sales ledger control account

20X7		£	20X7		£
01 Sep	Balance b/d	188,360	01 Sep	Balance b/d	2,140
30 Sep	Sales		30 Sep	Sales returns	9,160
	(101,260 + 1,360) (ii)	102,620		Cash received	91,270
	Cash refunds	300		Cash discounts	1,430
	Petty cash refund (iii)	20		Irrecoverable debts	460
	Balance c/d (W1)	3,320		Contras (480 + 500)	980
				Balance c/d	189,180
		294,620			294,620

Purchases ledger control account

20X7		£	20X7		£
01 Sep	Balance b/d	120	01 Sep	Balance b/d	89,410
30 Sep	Purchases returns	4,280	30 Sep	Purchases	
				(68,420 – 1,360) (ii)	67,060
	Cash to suppliers	71,840		Balance c/d	90
	Cash discounts	880			
	Contras (480 + 500)	980			
	Balance carried down	78,460			
		156,560			156,560

(W1) Sales ledger credit balances

	£
Draft closing balance	3,360
Wrong way adjustment of £20 refund	(40)
	3,320

18   SALLY

(a)   Journals

		Dr £	Cr £
(i)	Sally Ltd purchase ledger control	1,080	
	Sally Ltd sales ledger control (Being contra settlement)		1,080

(ii)	Irrecoverable debts expense	3,590	
	Sales ledger control (Being irrecoverable debts written off)		3,590

(iii)	Allowance for doubtful debts adjustment (5,200 – 3,060)	2,140	
	Allowance for doubtful debts (Being an increase in the allowance for doubtful debts)		2,140

(iv)	AUE Ltd sales ledger	200	
	AUT Ltd sales ledger (Being correction of misposted cash receipt)		200

(b) **Receivables**

	£
Sales ledger balance	384,600
Contra settlement (i)	(1,080)
Irrecoverable debt write offs (ii)	(3,590)
	————
	379,930
Less Allowance for doubtful debts (iii)	(5,200)
	————
Receivables	374,730
	————

19 GEORGE

(a) Annual depreciation charge $= £8,400 \times 15\%$

$= £1,260$

	£
Cost	8,400
Less: depreciation (1,260 × 19/12)	(1,995)
	————
Carrying amount	**6,405**
	————

The asset was owned for a total of 19 months between 1 May 20X0 and 1 December 20X1. As it was sold on the 1 December 20X1 i.e. at the beginning of the month, that month does not incur a depreciation charge. If the asset had been sold on the 31 December 20X1 there would be a month's depreciation for December 20X1.

(b) **Loss** on disposal $= £6,405 - £6,000$

$= £405$

A loss on disposal was made as the sales proceeds were £405 less than the carrying amount.

20 MATTRESS

Task 1

JOURNAL		Dr £	Cr £
(a)	Motor expenses	150	
	Motor vehicle at cost		150
(b)	Suspense	400	
	VAT (sales tax) account		400
(c)	Disposal account	11,000	
	Fixtures and fittings at cost		11,000
	Accumulated depreciation (F&F)	4,400	
	Disposal account		4,400
	Suspense	7,000	
	Disposal account		7,000
	Disposal account	400	
	Statement of profit or loss account (gain)		400
(d)	Suspense	3,600	
	Sales		3,600
(e)	Suspense	2,510	
	Bank		2,510

21 NCA 1

Account	Dr	Cr
Disposals	12,000	
Motor vehicles at cost		12,000
Motor vehicles accumulated depreciation	9,119	
Disposals		9,119
Motor vehicles at cost	15,250	
Motor vehicle expenses	210	
Disposals		3,800
Sundry payables		11,660
Totals	36,579	36,579

22 DAVE'S DOORS

(a) Year ended 31/12/X1 £20,000 × 10% = £2,000

Year ended 31/12/X2 (£20,000 – £2,000) × 10% = £1,800

Year ended 31/12/X3 (£20,000 – £2,000 – £1,800) × 10% = £1,620

Total accumulated depreciation (£2,000 + £1,800 + £1,620) = £5,420

(b)

Narrative	Dr	Cr
Disposals account	20,000	
Machinery cost account		20,000
Machinery accumulated depreciation account	5,420	
Disposals account		5,420
Bank	10,000	
VAT Control (20/120 × £10,000)		1,667
Disposals account (100/120 × £10,000)		8,333
Totals	35,420	35,420

Disposals

Machinery at cost	20,000	Machinery accumulated depreciation	5,420
		Bank	8,333
		Loss on disposal	6,247
	20,000		20,000

The profit or loss on disposal can also be calculated by comparing the sales proceeds to the carrying amount. The sales proceeds are £8,333 compared to a carrying amount of £14,580.

Therefore, a loss of £6,247 has been made.

23   JP BAKERY

(a)

	£	Debit	Credit
Accruals	4,820		4,820
Prepayments	2,945	2,945	
Motor expenses	572	572	
Administration expenses	481	481	
Light and heat	1,073	1,073	
Revenue	48,729		48,729
Purchases	26,209	26,209	
SLCA	5,407	5,407	
PLCA	3,090		3,090
Rent	45	45	
Purchase returns	306		306
Discounts allowed	567	567	
Capital	10,000		10,000

Loan	15,000		15,000
Interest paid	750	750	
Drawings	4,770	4,770	
Motor vehicles – cost	19,000	19,000	
Motor vehicle – accumulated depreciation	2,043		2,043
VAT control	2,995		2,995
Wages	20,000	20,000	
Suspense account		**5,164**	
Totals		86,983	86,983

(b)

		Dr £	Cr £
(i)	Suspense	5,000	
	Capital		5,000
(ii)	Suspense	385	
	Sales ledger control account		385
(iii)	VAT	193	
	Suspense		193
(iv)	Rent	9,000	
	Suspense		9,000
(v)	Electricity	1,356	
	Suspense		1,356

24   CONTROL LTD

(a)   £55,200

(b)   **Receivables (Sales ledger) control account**

Balance b/d	4,120	Bank	**53,610**
Credit sales (from part a)	55,200	Balance c/d	5,710
	59,320		59,320

(c)   £254,400

(d)   **Bank account**

Balance b/d	5,630	Payroll expenses	48,000
SLCA (from part b)	53,610	Administration expenses	6,400
Cash sales (from part c)	254,400	Vehicle running costs	192,000
		Drawings	41,800
		Sales tax	17,300
		Balance c/d	8,140
	313,640		313,640

25   BRIAN

Assets = Liabilities + Capital

£16,500 = £10,300 + (£3,700 - £1,500 + profit)

£16,500 = £10,300 + £2,200 + profit

Profit = £16,500 - £12,500 = **£4,000**

26   ELSIE

(a)   £1,280,000 × 75/100 = £960,000

(b)   £960,000 − (£970,200 − £98,006) = £87,806

27 FIVE SCENARIOS

Scenario 1

The principle of confidentiality imposes an obligation on Alessandro to refrain from

using the information to the advantage of Sueka LLP'	✓
disclosing the information within Sueka LLP'	
disclosing the information to anyone at Polina Ltd'	

Scenario 2

As she shows business acumen, offer her the job	
As she has breached the fundamental principles of integrity and confidentiality, report her to the AAT	✓
As she lacks integrity, inform her that she will not be offered the job	✓

Scenario 3

Objectivity and confidentiality	✓
Integrity and professional behaviour	
Confidentiality and professional competence	

Objectivity as Vernon has a conflict of interest – which is he representing?

Confidentiality as it would be very hard for Vernon not use the knowledge he has for one company when arguing for the other's position.

Scenario 4

Nothing	
Seek legal advice	
Advise Sam of relevant threats and safeguards that will protect Nick should he receive such an offer from Sam's organisation	✓
Immediately inform higher levels of management	

Scenario 5

	Yes	No
Continue with forging a relationship with the client		✓
Inform the client that without knowing the correct address the client/accountant relationship cannot be forged	✓	
Consider reporting the conversation to NCA	✓	

To comply with customer due diligence (part of money laundering regulations), the best course of action for Connor to take would be to inform the client that without knowing the correct address the client/accountant relationship cannot be forged.

The reluctance to disclose an address raises concerns over possible money laundering, so Connor must consider reporting the conversation to NCA.

28   JESS

(a)

Objectivity	
Integrity	
Confidentiality	
Professional behaviour	
Professional competence and due care	✓

(b)

Yes	
No	✓

This situation represents a threat to the fundamental principle of Technical Competency.

29   NIGHT OUT

(a)

Objectivity	
Integrity	
Confidentiality	
Professional behaviour	✓
Professional competence and due care	

(b)

Nothing	
Report the FD to the police	
Immediately inform the Managing Director	
Suggest to the Finance Director that the sign should be replaced, and possibly discuss the matter with the Managing Director	✓

30   RS

(a)   **A and D**

The fundamental principles of integrity and objectivity are being threated here. Changing the management information would breach both of these principles.

(b)   **D**

The offers of incentives make this a self-interest threat as RS stands to benefit if he/she changes the figures.

TASK 3 HUMAN ASSESSED

31   INVENTORY

(a)   **£10,800**

Using FIFO, inventory is issued at the earliest price.

The issue on the 19 January would be made up of 500 costing	1,250
1,000 costing	2,750
600 × £2.80	1,680
The issue on the 31 January would be made up of 1,000 × 2.80	2,800
800 × £2.90	2,320
Total issue value	**£10,800**

(b)   **£5,120**

Using LIFO, the 1,900 units of closing inventory is valued as the opening inventory of 500 units (£1,250) plus the 1,000 units received on 4 January (£2,750) plus 400 of the units received on 11 January, which have a value of £4,480 × 400/1,600 = £1,120.

	£
400 units of opening inventory	1,250
1,000 units received on 4 January	2,750
400 units received on 11 January	1,120
Total value of closing inventory	**5,120**

(c)   **£2.83**

With the average cost method, a new average cost only needs to be calculated before there is an issue from stores.

	Units	Total cost £	Average cost £
Opening inventory	500	1,250	
Receipts on 4 January	1,000	2,750	
Receipts on 11 January	1,600	4,480	
Receipts on 18 January	1,200	3,480	
	4,300	11,960	£2.78
Issues on 19 January	(2,100)	(5,838)	£2.78
	2,200	6,122	
Receipts on 25 January	1,500	4,350	
	3,700	10,472	**£2.83**
Issues on 31 January	(1,800)	(5,094)	**£2.83**
	1,900	5,378	

(d)   Unit prices are rising from £2.50 in the opening inventory, through £2.75 on 4/1, £2.80 on 11/1 and £2.90 on both 18/1 and 25/1. In this situation FIFO will generate a higher profit than AVCO or LIFO as more cost is transferred to the next accounting period in the closing inventory.

	FIFO	£	**AVCO**	£	**LIFO**	
Sales (illustrative figure)		15,000		15,000		15,000
Less: cost of sales						
Opening inventory	1,250		1,250		1,250	
Purchases	15,060		15,060		15,060	
Less: closing inventory	(5,510)		(5,378)		(5,120)	
		(10,800)		(10,932)		(11,190)
Gross profit		4,200		4,068		3,810

If costs were decreasing, then LIFO would give the higher profit. If there is no change in the unit price, then the profits would be the same regardless of the technique used.

32   LABOUR

Overtime is made up of two parts – the basic rate and the premium rate. Together they make up the total overtime payment. The basic rate is what the employee would receive for a normal working hour and the premium is an extra amount for working the extra hour.

The basic rate part of the overtime payment is classed as direct labour for direct employees. The premium part could be either direct or indirect depending on why the overtime is being worked. If the overtime can be attributed directly to production, i.e. at the specific request of a customer, then it can be classified as direct labour. If the overtime occurs due to general work pressures, then it would be classified as indirect labour.

33   AC V ABC

(a)   £35.00

$$\text{Overhead absorption rate} = \frac{\text{Total overhead cost}}{\text{Total number of direct labour hours}}$$

Total overhead cost = 90,000 + 150,000 + 180,000 = £420,000

Total direct labour hours = (5 × 1,200) + (5 × 10,800) = 60,000 direct labour hours

Overhead absorption rate = £420,000 ÷ 60,000 direct labour hours

Overhead absorption rate = £7.00 per labour hour

Alpha uses 5 direct labour hours per unit so will have an overhead cost per unit of 5 hours × £7.00 per hour = £35.00.

(b)   Activity based costing (ABC) is an alternative approach to product costing. It is a form of absorption costing but rather than absorbing overheads on a production volume basis, it firstly allocates them to cost pools before absorbing them into units using cost drivers.

A cost pool is an activity that consumes resources and for which overhead costs are identified and allocated. For each cost pool there should be a cost driver.

A cost driver is a unit of activity that consumes resources. An alternative definition of a cost driver is the factor influencing the level of cost.

(c)   ABC has a number of advantages:

- more accurate cost per unit. As a result, pricing, sales strategy, performance management and decision making should be improved

- better insight into what causes overhead costs

- overhead costs are not all related to production and sales volume

- overhead costs can be a significant proportion of total costs and overhead costs can be controlled by managing cost drivers

- applicable in a complex business environment

- can be applied to all overhead costs, not just production overheads

- can be used just as easily in service costing as in product costing.

Disadvantages of ABC:

- limited benefit if the overhead costs are a small proportion of the overall cost

- impossible to allocate all overhead costs to specific activities

- choice of both activities and cost drivers might be inappropriate

- more complex to explain

- benefits might not justify the costs.

34   MC V AC

When using marginal costing the cost of sales is valued at the variable production cost only and the fixed costs are a period charge. When using absorption costing the fixed production costs are absorbed into production so are included in the cost of sales. Only the non-production costs are a period charge.

There are 1,800kg produced but only 1,000kg are sold leaving 800kg in closing inventory.

Marginal costing - the production cost only includes the direct materials and labour = £25,200. The closing inventory is valued = £25,200/1,800 × 800 = £11,200. All the fixed production cost £3,600 is charged in the period.

Absorption costing - The production costs include the direct materials and labour and the fixed production overheads as well = £28,800. The fixed production cost per unit = £3,600/1,800kg = £2 per kg (OAR). The closing inventory is valued = £28,800/1,800 × 800 = £12,800. Unlike marginal costing not all of the fixed production cost is charged in the period. £2 × 800 = £1,600 of fixed cost is carried forward in the closing inventory to become part of the opening inventory cost in the next period. As there is no opening inventory in this forecast this accounts for the difference in the profits.

MC profit less AC profit = £30,390 - £31,990 = £1,600

35   CVP

(a)   **CVP analysis**

		Present	Proposed

(i)   Breakeven point

$$\text{Units} = \frac{\text{Fixed costs}}{\text{Contribution per unit}}$$

	Present	Proposed
	$\dfrac{96,000}{(1.70-1.40)}$	$\dfrac{130,000}{(1.60-1.35)}$
	= 320,000 units	= 520,000 units
Revenue: × 1.70/1.60	£544,000	£832,000

(ii)   Annual profit

	Present	Proposed
Sales units	500,000	750,000
Contribution per unit	£0.30	£0.25
	£	£
Total contribution	150,000	187,500
Fixed costs	96,000	130,000
Profit	54,000	57,500

(iii)   Margin of safety ratio

$$\frac{\text{Budgeted units} - \text{breakeven}}{\text{Budgeted units}}$$

	Present	Proposed
	$\dfrac{500-320}{500}$	$\dfrac{750-520}{750}$
	= 0.36 × 100 = 36%	= 0.307 × 100 = 30.7%

(b)   **Advice to Dilemma**

Looking at the figures alone, the advice to Dilemma would be to proceed with the proposed expansion, as it is projected to increase annual profits by £3,500, i.e. 6.5%.

Note: the margin of safety ratio (the relative amount by which sales can fall below budget before making a loss) will fall from 36% to 30.7%.

This means that the business could be more vulnerable to downturns in the market.

36   LF

(a)

	Product			
	A	B	C	D
Selling price	100	110	120	120
Variable cost per unit	54	55	59	66
Contribution/unit	£46.00	£55.00	£61.00	£54.00
Hours/unit $\left(\dfrac{\text{Direct labour cost}}{£6/\text{hour}}\right)$	3.00	2.50	4.00	4.50
Contribution/hour	£15.33	£22.00	£15.25	£12.00
Ranking	2nd	1st	3rd	4th

Product	Litres	Labour hours used	Total contribution £
B	150	375	8,250
A	200	600	9,200
C	92	370	5,612
D	0	0	0
Total Contribution			23,062
Less: Fixed costs (W1)			12,800
Profit			10,262

(W1) OAR per hour (using product A as an example) = £24/3 hours = £8. Overhead for the period = £8 × 1,600 hours = £12,800

(b) This is an example of Limiting Factor analysis. The direct labour hours have been identified as the limiting factor as there will not be enough hours available to produce the maximum demand for all four products.

When a limiting factor is identified the best use of the limited resource needs to be identified. In this case identify which product will make the most contribution per labour hour.

When making a short term decision, marginal costing techniques are used. Firstly, calculate the contribution and then calculate how much contribution is made per labour hour required to make the product. The products are then ranked to create the production plan from best to worst with the best making the most contribution per labour hour.

37 FLEXED BUDGETS

(a)

	£
Sales revenue 64,800/2,160 × 2,700	81,000
Direct materials 9,720/2,160 × 2,700	12,150
Direct labour 22,680/2,160 × 2,700	28,350
Fixed overheads	12,960
Semi-variable costs (W1)	7,884
Total cost	61,344
Total profit	19,656
Profit per unit (to 2 decimal places)	7.28

(W1)

$$\text{VC per unit} = \frac{£13,284 - £6,804}{5,400 - 2,160} = £2.00$$

FC = £13,284 - (5,400 × £2.00) = £2,484

TC at 2,700 units = £2,484 + (2,700 × £2.00) = £7,884

(b)   Sales revenue and the direct costs all have a variable behaviour. This means that as activity increases the total cost or revenue increases in direct proportion. A variable behaviour means that the cost or revenue per unit is constant. To be able to flex the budget it is possible to calculate the cost or revenue per unit at the original activity level and use this at the new activity level. For example – direct materials £9,720/2,160 gives a variable cost per unit of £4.50. This is assumed to stay constant as the activity level increases to 2,700 units so the total cost is £4.50 × 2,700 = £12,150.

Fixed costs are assumed to remain constant in total as activity levels change, unless told otherwise. So at 2,160 units the fixed cost was £12,960 and it should remain so at the new activity level of 2,700 units.

Semi-variable costs have a fixed element and a variable element. To separate them the high-low method is used. It is assumed that the only thing causing the change in the cost is the change in activity level. First calculate the variable cost per unit based on the change in cost being divided by the change in activity. This value is then used to calculate the total variable cost at one of the activity levels. Once this is known it can be deducted from the total cost to calculate the fixed cost. These can then be treated as mentioned above to calculate the total semi-variable cost at the new activity level. The variable cost per unit is multiplied by the new activity level and then added to the fixed cost to give the total cost.

(c)   The profit per unit will drop as activity levels increase, assuming that the variable cost per unit and the total fixed cost remain constant. This means that as the activity levels increase the fixed cost is shared over more units and becomes cheaper per unit. As the fixed cost becomes cheaper per unit the profit per unit will increase.

38   VARIANCES

Materials variance

The general price of materials may have fallen since the budget was set. The new machinery is likely to manufacture the finished product more effectively with less waste. Similarly, the new highly skilled labour will be able to handle the raw materials more effectively with less waste. This would lead to a favourable variance.

Labour variances

The new higher skilled workers will be paid a higher hourly rate. The redundancy costs for the less skilled workers may have been included in this month's wages costs. Both would lead to an adverse variance.

But higher skilled workers will be more efficient overall, capable of producing more components per hour. They may also be highly motivated as they had just been recruited to new roles. These would lead to a favourable variance counteracting the adverse variance.

Fixed overhead variances

Some of the favourable variance can be explained by the reduction in rent and the lower depreciation charge on the new machinery. Both would have reduced overall fixed overhead expenditure in comparison to the original budget.

The efficiency of the new machine could improve productive capacity. Coupled with the higher skilled labour, which is likely to be able to produce more in their working week, more units would have been produced than expected. Increasing the favourable variance further.

39   INVESTMENT APPRAISAL

(a)

Investment	Option 1	Option 2	Option 3	Option 4
1	✓			
2				✓

(b)   For the first investment Loft Lifting Ltd should invest in option 1 as it has the shortest payback period. Payback period measures how long it takes to recoup the initial cost of an investment. The shorter the payback period the more confident we are in the accuracy of the cash flows used in the calculation. The more certain we are the less risky the investment is seen to be.

For the second investment Loft Lifting Ltd should invest in option 4 as it has the highest NPV. The NPV measures the net present value of the investment. The net present value is the return the investment should give over the whole life of the investment and also take into account the time value of money by discounting the cash flows. The higher the NPV, the more return there should be for the shareholders of Loft Lifting Ltd.

TASK 4 HUMAN ASSESSED

40   DILIGENCE

(a)   To comply with customer due diligence (part of money laundering regulations), the best course of action for Connor to take would be to inform the client that without knowing the correct address the client/accountant relationship cannot be forged.

(b)   The reluctance to disclose an address raises concerns over possible money laundering, so Connor must consider reporting the conversation to NCA.

41   REFERENCE

(a)   The ethical principles involved here are as follows:

- **Integrity** – Steve must be straightforward and honest in all professional and business relationships. Integrity also implies fair dealing and truthfulness and there is a danger that the reference is not a fair or true representation of the facts as he sees them.

- **Objectivity** – the large fee should not be allowed to colour Steve's judgement. This presents a self-interest threat.

    It could also be argued that, because Kept Ltd is Steve's oldest client, there is also a familiarity threat to objectivity.

- **Professional behaviour** – writing a reference that Steve suspects to be false could bring discredit to himself and the profession.

(b)   Steve is potentially guilty of 'fraud by false representation' under the Fraud Act 2006. This is where a person makes 'any representation as to fact or law ... express or implied' which they know to be untrue or misleading.

There is also the possibility that the large fee could be interpreted as a bribe under the Bribery Act 2010 and Steve could be found guilty of passive bribery (receiving a bribe) under the Act.

(c)   It is acceptable practice for Steve to include a disclaimer of liability and it certainly does no harm to include one. However, disclaimers can be challenged in court so may not afford Steve any protection.

If he has serious doubts over whether or not Kept Ltd will be able to pay the rent, then he shouldn't write the reference.

42   CYCLE

(a)   Mthbe needs to keep up-to-date in the following areas (only TWO needed):

- tax legislation/compliance
- money laundering regulations
- accounting/reporting standards
- regulation of accounting.

The reasons for this are as follows:

- They are important areas because clients are businesses, which must comply with requirement for accurate accounts preparation and tax returns.
- Mthbe needs to ensure he is technically competent to undertake the work (fundamental principle of professional competence and due care).
- Mthbe needs to protect himself with regards to money laundering.

(b)   The AAT CPD policy asks Mthbe to update his skills twice a year.

(c)   The AAT's CPD cycle has four stages – assess, plan, action and evaluation.

43   SARAH

(a)   Sarah should obtain authority from the client to give the financial information.

(b)   It is not possible to give an assurance regarding the client ability to pay the rent.

44   KUTCHINS

Gemma is allowed to use general knowledge and experience from a previous employer but NOT specific information from that employer that is covered by the duty of confidentiality.

This means that general accountancy, audit and management skills and knowledge can all be used but not specific information concerning Kirk Ltd.

45   BEVIS

Matter 1

Bevis should NOT tell the Managing Director anything that would be considered 'private information' as this would be a breach of confidentiality.

Matter 2

Bevis should tell the customer that he has been unable to gain the information. Pretending to be a customer lacks integrity and would not be acting professionally.

46 DILEMMA

(a) Confidentiality.

(b) You should not tell your friend about the redundancies as to do so would breach confidentiality.

47 JUSTIN

(a) This situation presents a self-interest threat.

(b) The best course of action is for Justin to declare his intent and then to remove Justin from this assurance engagement.

48 JULIE

(a) This situation presents a self-interest threat.

(b) Two safeguards the assurance firm should have in place are:

- A policy requiring the immediate disclosure of such an offer of employment

- A policy requiring Julie to be removed from the assurance engagement.

49 NO DEFENCE

(a) The Bribery Act 2010 creates four offences:

1 bribing a person to induce or reward them to perform a relevant function improperly

2 requesting, accepting or receiving a bribe as a reward for performing a relevant function improperly

3 using a bribe to influence a foreign official to gain a business advantage

4 a new form of corporate liability for failing to prevent bribery on behalf of a commercial organisation.

(b) For a commercial organisation, it is a defence to have in place 'adequate procedures' to prevent bribery.

This may include implementing anti-bribery procedures.

It is important that firms consider what procedures are 'adequate' for their firm given the risks they face and the way they run their business. The procedures should be proportionate to the risk posed.

For some firms there will be no need to put bribery prevention procedures in place as there is no risk of bribery on their behalf. Other firms may need to put measures in place in key areas, such as gifts and hospitality, as this is the area where they have identified a risk.

Corporate ignorance of individual wrongdoing will provide no protection against prosecution.

(c) Certainly the excessive nature of the hospitality would mean that it would be viewed as an attempt to bribe the MP concerned.

While M plc could argue that they are not guilty of 1, 2 and 3 above, they are likely to be found guilty under offence 4.

Even though Mr Igbinadola was an agent and not an employee and even though the Board claim ignorance, the company could still be found guilty of failing to prevent bribery.

The only possible defence would be to demonstrate that they had adequate procedures in place to prevent bribery, but in this case it looks difficult to prove this.

50   L PLC

Arguing that an activity complies with 'local law' or 'customs and practices' is not a defence under the Bribery Act.

If L plc goes ahead with the request, then two offences under the Act will have been committed:

1   Using a bribe (the donations) to influence a foreign official to gain a business advantage.

2   Failing to prevent bribery on behalf of a commercial organisation.

L plc should thus refuse the request for 'donations'.

51   IN-HOUSE CODE

The code is a voluntary one prepared by John Grooms Ltd for its own use.

It cannot insist on suppliers adopting it.

The code cannot be statutory since that would be created under legislation/regulation/ case law and used by many companies. It therefore has no legal status.

52   NEW CODE

1   **All products should be purchased from local farms and suppliers where appropriate.**

This would have a positive impact from a sustainability perspective as it would reduce distribution miles and the associated impact on fossil fuels and pollution.

The main reservation is the wording 'where appropriate' as there is no indication as to what 'appropriate' means – for example, Cosby could buy cheaper goods from overseas suppliers and argue that the low cost made it 'appropriate'.

2   **All packing materials should be obtained from renewable sources where feasible.**

This would also have a positive impact from a sustainability perspective as it would reduce deforestation to provide cardboard and paper packaging.

The main reservation is the wording 'where feasible' as there is no indication as to what 'feasible' means – for example, Cosby could buy cheaper goods with plastic packaging and argue that the low cost made it 'feasible'.

3   All suppliers to be paid on time.

This should mean that suppliers are treated fairly. However, there is no indication that suppliers have any say in what constitutes 'on time'.

4   All suppliers to be paid fair prices as determined by the Purchasing Manager.

This should also mean that suppliers are treated fairly.

However, there is no indication that suppliers have any say in what constitutes 'fair prices' – the price needs to be seen to be reasonable and fair by both parties.

53   PROCEDURE

(a)   Ye Lin must cooperate fully with the investigation.

(b)   If Ye Lin fails to cooperate as an AAT member she could be found guilty of misconduct.

(c)   The AAT could apply the following disciplinary actions:

- be expelled from the Association

- have her membership of the Association suspended

- have her practicing licence withdrawn.

54   CHRIS

(a)   This situation represents a threat to the fundamental principles of:

- Objectivity – because it is difficult to act without a perception of bias when the two clients' interests are in such conflict because they both want a price and terms beneficial to themselves; and

- Confidentiality – because he has confidential information in respect of each client.

(b)   Chris should:

- consider relevant facts/ethical issues involved/his fundamental principles/any established procedures in HJK and Co

- establish alternative courses of action, establish which is most consistent with the fundamental principles and establish the consequences of each

- seek advice about the matter within HJK and Co, and document the substance of the issue and discussions.

(c)   In acting for one of the clients Chris should consider instituting appropriate safeguards so that his familiarity with the other client does not affect his professional judgement/objectivity, and so that he does not breach confidentiality with regards to the other party.

55   SIMON

(a)   This situation represents a self-interest threat.

(b)   Simon's best course of action is to sell the shares or, failing that, to ask to be removed from the audit engagement.

56   LAST

(a)   This situation displays a breach of confidentiality.

(b)   Jason's friend, Brian, should talk to the director concerned and explained that to act in the way suggested would be unethical.

(**Note:** you could have answered that he should get advice without breaching confidentiality, say by ringing the AAT ethics helpline.)

(c)   Brian should resign and state the reason for the resignation. Then report the situation to the external regulators.

57   SAFE AND SOUND

Matter A

The ethical threat is basically one of self-interest.

The director is using price sensitive information to ensure that a loss is prevented by selling shares now rather than after the announcement of poor results for the company.

One ethical safeguard would be a professional code of conduct that requires directors to carry out their duties with integrity and therefore in the best interests of the shareholders. The director would recognise that selling the shares would start the share price falling already and this would not benefit the shareholders.

As a code it may not be effective – the director could argue that selling shares prior to the results was designed to warn shareholders of the imminent fall in share price and was, therefore, in their best interests.

An alternative course of action is to ban trading in shares a given number of weeks prior to the announcement of company results (as happens in the USA where directors are not allowed to sell shares during 'blackout periods'). This would be effective as share sales can be identified and the directors could incur a penalty for breach of legislation.

Matter B

The ethical threat appears to be a lack of independence and self-interest regarding the setting of remuneration for these directors.

Not only do they have common directorships, but they are also good friends. They could easily vote for higher than normal remuneration packages for each other on the remuneration committees knowing that the other director will reciprocate on the other remuneration committee.

In corporate governance terms, one ethical safeguard is to ban these cross-directorships.

The ban would be enforceable as the directors of companies must be stated in the annual accounts, hence it would be easy to identify cross-directorships. The ban would also be effective as the conflict of interest would be removed.

In professional terms, the directors clearly have a conflict of interest. While their professional code of ethics may mention this precisely as an ethical threat, Graham and Mike should follow the spirit of the code and resign their non-executive directorships. This again would remove the threat.

Matter C

There is a clear ethical threat to the directors of Company Z.

They appear to be being bribed so that they do not query the management style of the chairman. The threat is that the directors will simply accept the benefits given to them rather than try to run Company Z in the interests of the shareholders. It is clearly easy to accept that option.

Ethical safeguards are difficult to identify and their application depends primarily on the desire of the directors to take ethical actions. In overall terms, the chairman does not appear to be directly breaching ethical or governance codes. The main safeguard is therefore for the directors not to accept appointment as director to Company Z or resign from the board if already a director.

The director could attempt to get the matter discussed at board level, although it is unlikely the chairman would allow this. Taking any other action is in effect 'whistle blowing' on all the directors and has the negative impact that the director would also have to admit to receiving 'benefits' from the company.

58 FREE HOLIDAYS

The Bribery Act 2010 creates four offences:

1   bribing a person to induce or reward them to perform a relevant function improperly

2   requesting, accepting or receiving a bribe as a reward for performing a relevant function improperly

3   using a bribe to influence a foreign official to gain a business advantage

4   a new form of corporate liability for failing to prevent bribery on behalf of a commercial organisation.

Leigh Davis is guilty of bribery (offence 1 above) under the Act as he is bribing Sarah by offering her free holidays in return for her performing her function as an audit manager improperly.

Sarah is guilty of receiving a bribe (offence 2 above) from Leigh Davis.

B & Sons LLP could also be guilty of bribery of the Act for failing to prevent bribery (offence 4 above) unless they can show that they had in place 'adequate procedures'.

Both Leigh and Sarah could receive a maximum jail sentence of up to ten years.

If B & Sons LLP is found guilty they could be liable for an unlimited fine.

59 KEN

(a)   Money laundering is the process by which the proceeds of crime, either money or other property, are converted into assets, which appear to have a legitimate rather than an illegal origin. The aim of the process is to disguise the source of the property, in order to allow the holder to enjoy it free from suspicion as to its source.

The Proceeds of Crime Act 2002 (POCA) seeks to control money laundering by creating three categories of criminal offences in relation to the activity.

Laundering

Under the POCA, the three money laundering offences are

- s327 – Concealing, disguising, converting, transferring or removing criminal property.

- s328 – Taking part in an arrangement to facilitate the acquisition, use or control of criminal property.

- s329 – Acquiring, using or possessing criminal property.

These offences are punishable on conviction by a maximum of 14 years' imprisonment and/or a fine.

Failure to report

The second category of offence relates to failing to report a knowledge or suspicion of money laundering. It is an offence for a person who knows or suspects that another person is engaged in money laundering not to report the fact to the appropriate authority.

However, the offence only relates to individuals, such as accountants, who are acting in the course of business in the regulated sector.

The offences set out in these sections are punishable on conviction by a maximum of five years' imprisonment and/or a fine.

Tipping off

The third category of offence relates to tipping off. It is an offence to make a disclosure which is likely to prejudice any investigation under the Act.

The offences set out in these sections are punishable on conviction by a maximum of two years' imprisonment and/or a fine.

(b)   Ken would therefore be guilty of the primary offence of money laundering as explained in the section above.

Los is also guilty of an offence in relation to the Proceeds of Crime Act as he is clearly assisting Ken in his money laundering procedure. He is actively concealing and disguising criminal property, and his arrangement with Ken facilitates the retention of criminal property.

Mel is equally guilty under the same provisions as Los, in that he is actively engaged in the money laundering process, by producing false accounts.

60   MLRO

(a)   Jeff has just committed the offence of tipping off.

(b)   The maximum sentence is two years.

(c)   In the absence of an MLRO, Jeff should have approached NCA with his concerns.

(d)   De minimus means no minimum limit.

61 ADAM

Matter 1

Adam is obliged to report this refusal to disclose and the information surrounding it to the firm's Money Laundering Reporting Officer (MLRO).

Matter 2

This scenario also gives grounds for suspicion of money laundering. Why doesn't the client, H Ltd, simply want LOFT to repay them and then it up to them whether they want to pay anything to Q Ltd? Is it to make funds difficult to trace, so 'dirty cash' becomes a nice clean cheque from a reputable accounting firm?

Any overpayment by a customer should be thoroughly investigated by a senior member of finance function staff and only repaid to the customer once it has been established that it is right/legal to do so.

Similarly, the request to pay a third party should be scrutinised before any payment is agreed to. Without further information the transaction does not make commercial sense.

Unless investigations satisfy any concerns raised, then LOFT should refuse the payment and the MRLO should fill in a Suspicious Activity Report (SAR) to be sent to the NCA.

62 DONNA

Funds dishonestly retained after discovery of a tax error become criminal property so their retention amounts to money laundering by Stoppard plc.

As she is now aware of the error, Donna should report to the National Crime Agency (NCA) that she suspects Stoppard plc of money laundering because it has refused to notify the matter to HMRC. She will be protected from a claim for breach of confidentiality when making this report.

Knowing she may have been involved in money laundering, Donna needs to make an authorised disclosure to NCA which may help protect her from a charge that she herself, in making the error, was engaged in money laundering.

63 DUMPING

Members have a duty of confidentiality.

However, there are occasions where the accountant has a professional or legal duty to disclose the information and therefore the breach of confidentiality is permissible.

Environmental damage is one such instance.

64 INTEGRITY

Appropriate responses include the following:

Internal action

- Discuss the matter with the Finance Director to see if there is a valid case for posting this journal. From the information given, this seems unlikely.

External action

If the FD refuses to change the request and Frankie still feels uncomfortable, then he could:

- Go to the company's auditors to discuss the matter

- Seek guidance from the AAT.

Ultimately if the situation is not resolved, then he should consider resigning.

Note: The wrong answer here is to suggest that he should post the journal without question as the Finance director is his senior. This is NOT an appropriate action.

65   BENEFITS

(a)   The ethical principles potentially affected are as follows:

Integrity – How will Jacqui manage her personal interest with the need to be true and fair?

Objectivity – How will Jacqui manage her personal interest in the benefits package with the need to remain unbiased and consider only the relevant facts?

Professional Competence and Due Care – Does Jacqui have all the necessary skills to draw up such a package?

Professional Behaviour – How should Jacqui proceed so as not to bring discredit herself and the accountancy profession?

It would be very easy for Jacqui's recommendations to appear biased, even if she has acted ethically.

(b)   Jacqui should start by considering the following issues:

Identify relevant facts:

She should consider the organisation's policies, procedures and guidelines, accounting standards, best practices, code of ethics, applicable laws and regulations.

Is the information used for assessing the potential new benefits package independent? Who else has been involved in the proposal for the new benefits package?

Identify affected parties:

Key affected parties are Jacqui and the rest of the SMT. Other possible affected parties are employees, human resources, shareholders and financial backers.

Identify who should be involved in the resolution:

Jacqui should consider not just who should be involved, but also for what reason and timing of their involvement.

She could think about contacting the AAT for advice and guidance, or discuss the matter with trusted colleagues or someone from human resources.

(c)   **Possible courses of action**

Before explaining her findings to the SMT, it may be advisable for Jacqui to tell the SMT how she approached the project and who else was involved, for example, human resources.

She should declare her conflict of interest and not vote on the proposal for the new benefits package.

It may be advisable to involve human resources or another independent party to present the findings to the SMT. During the presentation, she should demonstrate how her findings were arrived at and who else was involved in the project.

66 SUSHIL

(a) This situation presents an intimidation threat.

(b) The best course of action would be to speak to his employer and explain that it is illegal to falsify the accounts.

67 TRUE

(a) No, Naills as an AAT member has a duty to produce a true and fair view of the accounts.

(b) The definition of false accounting is concealing or falsifying accounting records with a view to personal gain or providing false information that is misleading or deceptive.

68 MEERA

Matter 1

(a) **Fees**

While some discounting of fees is seen as commercially acceptable way to win business, heavily discounted fees are perceived as a 'self-interest' threat to professional behaviour. This does not mean that they should be avoided at all costs but guidelines need to be followed.

Fees should reflect the value of the professional services performed for the client and there is a risk with low fees of a perception that the quality of work could be impaired.

Tax bill

Meera should consider the fundamental principle of Integrity.

It would be dishonest to promise to reduce a tax bill simply to gain a client when she believes the bill to be reasonable.

Matter 2

(b) Meera should continue to advise Greg to contact the HMRC but it would be a breach of confidentiality for her to do so without his express permission, which seems unlikely in this case.

(c) If Greg, after having had a reasonable time to reflect, does not correct the error, Meera should do the following:

- Inform Greg that she/her firm can no longer act for him because funds dishonestly retained after discovery of a tax error become criminal property so their retention amounts to money laundering by Greg.

- Make an internal report on the matter to her firm's MLRO.

69   DISMISS

The Public Interest Disclosure Act 1998 (PIDA) protects individuals from dismissal who disclose confidential information, whether internally or to a prescribed regulator when given in good faith.

Sarah is thus protected under the PIDA.

70   SUSTENANCE

(a)   **The role of accountants**

The roles of professional accountants in contributing to sustainability include the following:

- Challenging conventional assumptions of doing business.

- Redefining success.

- Establishing appropriate performance targets.

- Encouraging and rewarding the right behaviours.

- Ensuring that information flows that support decisions, and which monitor and report performance, go beyond the traditional ways of thinking about economic success.

Being sustainable requires the organisation to take full account of its impact on the planet and its people.

(b)   **Impact on profit**

An increased emphasis on sustainability can result in improved profits for the following reasons:

- Potential cost savings – e.g. due to lower energy usage.

- Short term gain in sales – e.g. if customers are influenced by sustainability-related labels on products.

- Long term gain in sales – e.g. due to enhanced PR and reputation.

- Better risk management – e.g. pre-empting changes in regulations may save compliance costs.

71   HOGGS FURNITURE

(a)   Sustainable development is defined as 'development that meets the needs of the present without compromising the ability of future generations to meet their own needs' (The UN's Bruntland Report).

Sustainability is thus more than just looking at environmental concerns. It relates to the continuity of **economic**, **social** and **environmental** aspects of human society.

Another way of looking at this is that sustainable businesses offer products and services that fulfil society's needs while placing an equal emphasis on people, planet and profits.

(b)   Areas that Jacob should appraise in order to answer the client's concerns include the following:

- Whether non-renewable hard woods are used in manufacture.

    The client would want reassurance that all materials are form renewable sources.

- The energy efficiency and level of emission of greenhouse gases due to the operation of the factory.

    While these cannot be eliminated altogether, the client would want to see evidence that Hoggs has taken steps to improve energy efficiency (e.g. thermal insulation, double glazing, installation of solar panels, etc) or uses carbon offset schemes.

- Treatment of staff

    Sustainability is not just about environmental issues but also incorporates social (people) aspects. The client may want to know what Hoggs' record is concerning accidents, staff development, diversity, etc.

- Tax

    Economic sustainability includes factors such as whether the company is paying tax and so contributing to the local/national community.

(c)   Other ways Jacob can contribute to sustainability through his role as an accountant includes the following:

- Helping create an ethics-based culture in Hoggs.

- By championing and promoting sustainability.

- By highlighting the risks of not acting sustainably and draw attention to reputational and other ethical risks.

- By incorporating targets and performance measures consistent with a Triple Bottom Line (TBL) approach.

72   MLC

MLC have clearly positioned themselves as an ethical company and will therefore attract shareholders who are looking for ethical investments and customers looking for ethically produced goods.

If they continue trading with this supplier then their reputation will suffer if the news gets out.

By taking strong decisive action and controlling the news story they have demonstrated that they follow their stated ethical principles.

The best response would thus be to "Cancel all contracts with the supplier and release a press statement stating how the company will always act quickly and decisively if unethical practices are suspected."

73 STEPHANIE

Integrity

Integrity implies that a person should be straightforward and honest in all business relationships. The management accountant is not being honest because he is helping to produce budgets he knows to be inaccurate.

Objectivity

By taking the football tickets in exchange for altering figures the management accountant is allowing bias to override business judgements.

Professional behaviour

The management accountant has not behaved professionally and in line with AAT expectations. In addition to using incorrect figures in the budgets he has tried to influence Stephanie to do the same.

Note: Professional competence and due care and Confidentiality have not been breached

The management accountant's skills are not under question and so this principle does not appear to have been breached. The management accountant does not appear to have breached confidentiality. The conversations Stephanie overheard involved Alpha staff and so no information has been leaked.

74 STEVEN

In respect of a genuine oversight, be it yours or a colleague's, AAT's code of ethics recognises that this can happen as long as the issue is promptly addressed and safeguards put in place.

It is possible to add an addendum about the incorrect note and this is the most appropriate action.

However, it would be advisable first to consult with N&Q Ltd's auditors for their guidance on how best to proceed.

If the accounts do not "represent the facts accurately and completely in all material respects" you should not sign them, nor should the MD.

75 INTEGRITY

Appropriate responses include the following:

Internal action

- Discuss the matter with the Finance Director to see if there is a valid case for posting this journal. From the information given, this seems unlikely.

External action

If the FD refuses to change the request and Frankie still feels uncomfortable, then he could:

- Go to the company's auditors to discuss the matter
- Seek guidance from the AAT.

Ultimately if the situation is not resolved, then he should consider resigning.

Note: The wrong answer here is to suggest that he should post the journal without question as the Finance director is his senior. This is NOT an appropriate action.

76 FINANCE

Option 1

Difference 1 – Limited liability – with a company a shareholder's liability is limited to any sums unpaid on shares issued, whereas with a partnership the partners are fully liable for business debts.
Difference 2 – Regulation / administration – companies must comply with the Companies Act and register with Companies House. Regulations for partnerships are less onerous
Difference 3 – Taxation – companies pay tax on the company's profits whereas partnership profits are split between partners according to a profit sharing ratio and added to partners' individual taxable income.
Implication for finance 1 – The limited liability that a company has may make it easier to attract potential shareholders than potential partners as they will perceive the investment to be less risky.
Implication for finance 2 – It's easier to spread ownership across a wide number of owners through issuing shares, rather than admitting new partners every time, again making attracting investors and raising finance easier.

Option 2

THREE elements of a SOFP that a bank would be interested in and why

Aspect of SOFP	Reason why the bank would look at this
1 Non-current assets	To assess whether the business has sufficient quality assets (e.g. land and buildings) to offer as security on a new loan. If it hasn't, then the bank may either refuse the loan or insist on higher interest rates to compensate for the extra risk.
2 Net current assets / liabilities	To asses liquidity and, therefore, the business's ability to pay loan interest and repayments
3 Loans	If a business already has a high level of loans (gearing), then the bank may feel it is too risky to lend it additional loans.

THREE stakeholders (other than a bank) who would use a SOFP and why

Stakeholder	Reason why they would use the SOFP
1 Potential suppliers	To assess the firm's ability to pay its creditors by looking at liquidity and, therefore, to decide whether or not to grant it credit.
2 Potential customers	To assess the financial stability of the business to evaluate its long term prospects before committing to any long term contracts.
3 Existing shareholders / owners	To assess the value of their investment in the business – for example, to assess whether the business could afford them taking out drawings or paying out a dividend.
4 Potential investors	To assess the financial stability of the business to help decide whether or not to invest.

Note: only three required

77 ACCOUNTING FUNDAMENTALS

1 The accounting equation

The accounting equation is as follows:

Assets – Liabilities = Capital + Profit – Drawings

Or rearranged:

Assets = Liabilities + Capital + Profit – Drawings

The equation is important as it is testing the basic principles of double entry- if the double entry has been done correctly (i.e. each transaction has at least 2 effects) then the equation will always balance.

If you look at the second equation above you can see that the equation is the same as the Balance sheet/ Statement of Financial position. So the accounting equation is being used to check double entry and to also produce the SOFP.

2 The statement of profit and loss

The statement of profit and loss (SOPL) shows how well a business has performed over a period of time. It compares revenue earned (i.e. sales) with various expenses incurred to calculate the overall profit for a period. This is usually for a year but can be different.

The first section of the profit or loss is called the trading section as it shows the pure profit from the trade of the business (i.e. sales less costs of sales = gross profit). Beneath the gross profit all the expenses of the business are deducted to give the net profit for the year.

The SOPL is produced using the accruals/matching basis, so for example we compare sales with costs of goods sold in order to calculate gross profit. Another example is where expenses incurred (for example telephone) are charged to the SOPL even though we may not have paid for them. This is so that the SOPL can accurately show all the revenues earned in a year and match them against the expenses incurred in a year (regardless of whether the cash has been paid/ received)

The SOPL is important as it informs the users of accounts as to whether the business has been successful in making profit for the period. It also (as mentioned above) shows whether the profit from the pure trade (gross profit) is sufficient to cover the expenses of the business.

It is used by different users or stakeholders of a business in making decisions. For example investors may choose to invest in a business that is making healthy profits. Or a bank may decide to lend to a business that is making healthy profits as it is confident that it will receive the interest payments.

3 The statement of financial position

The Statement of Financial position (SOFP) provides a snapshot of a business's strength or financial position at one point in time. This is usually at the end of the year.

It lists the assets of the business – these are split between non-current assets (for examples land and buildings that the business expects to use over more than a year) and also current assets (for example inventory and cash). The SOFP also lists amounts owed/ liabilities and these are also split between noncurrent liabilities and current liabilities. The non-current liabilities are those due after more than 1 year (for example a 10 year bank loan) and the current liabilities are due within a year (i.e. trade payables). The SOFP also shows the capital section which are amounts due back to the owner. As per the accounting equation the capital section will show capital + profit – drawings.

The SOFP is important as it shows the assets / liabilities position at one point in time. (It also shows the amount owed back to the owner i.e. capital). It shows the financial strength of the business (i.e. do the assets exceed liabilities?). It also shows how the business has been financed (i.e. has the bank lent the business a large amount of money?) It also shows the liquidity position of the business (see below).

It is used by different stakeholders/ users of the accounts to make decisions. For example, a bank may look at the business SOFP and see that it already has a large loan liability on the SOFP and therefore refuse further loans. The SOFP also shows the liquidity position of a business. By looking at the level of current assets and current liabilities it is easy to assess whether a business is liquid- i.e. does it have sufficient current assets to pay its bills as they fall due.

4 Comparing the SOPL and SOFP

Similarities:

Both the SOFP and SOPL are produced for external users (usually once a year). They are both prepared using the accruals/ matching concept and the going concern concept.

An example of the accruals concept would be telephone expense incurred but not paid would be shown as an expense in the SOPL. The amount not paid would be shown as an accrual in the SOFP.

The going concern concept also assumes that the business will continue to trade for the foreseeable future.

Finally both the SOPL and SOFP will be prepared under accounting standards - for example IAS 16 Property, plant and equipment.

Differences

The SOFP is showing the assets/ liabilities/ capital position on one day only i.e. the end of the financial year.

By contrast the SOPL shows the results of the business over, usually, the last 12 months (i.e. all the revenue/income and expenses from Jan to December)

Advantages

As mentioned above the SOPL and SOFP provide useful information to the users of accounts which they will then use to make decisions. These decisions include for investors, whether to invest in a business, for banks whether to lend money to the business. For suppliers, whether to offer credit terms to a business.

Disadvantages

Both the SOPF and SOPL report on past performance i.e. on results already happened and this may not be a reflection of what will happen in the future.

The accounts are prepared under accounting standards and this often involves a choice i.e. straight line and reducing balance depreciation and this could perhaps lead to manipulation of the accounts.

The SOFP also shows the cash position at the year-end but does not explain exactly where this cash has come from or what it has been spent on.

The SOFP also shows some items at historical cost i.e. land may be shown in the accounts at the amount paid, not the amount it is currently worth.

The SOFP also does not show any internally generated assets such as the goodwill/ reputation of the business.

78   CASH

THREE reasons why the net profit of a business for a period is not necessarily the same as the net cash generated in the same period.

Reason 1 – Timing differences

Timing difference are when the same figure eventually affects both profit and cash to the same degree but the timing is different. Examples:

- If sales of £1,000 are made in a month, then we expect to receive £1,000 cash but the customer may not pay for some months afterwards due to being given a credit period. The difference between sales and cash will be via receivables.

- Similarly if items of inventory are purchased, then the cost only impacts profit when the items are sold. If still in the warehouse, then the cost gets carried forward as closing inventory. The cash will be paid after receiving an invoice and waiting a given credit period.

Reason 2 – Items that affect profit but have no cash impact

Some items affect profit but do not have a cash implication. Examples:

- Depreciation reduces profit but is not a cash flow. (The long term cash equivalent would relate to buying/selling assets.)

- Another example would be making an allowance for receivables – these are recognised as an expense in the profit and loss account but the other side of the double entry is to reduce the receivables balance in the statement of financial position. There is no cash impact.

Reason 3 – Items that affect cash but do not affect profit

Finally, some items impact cash but do not go through the profit and loss account and do not affect profit.

Examples

- Owners taking drawings out of the business would reduce cash but are seen as an appropriation of profit rather than an expense.

- Similarly, payment of a dividend may reduce cash and use up retained profits but does not affect net profit for the period.

- Taking out or repaying a loan will impact cash but the other side of the double entry is on the statement of financial position not the profit and loss account.

TASK 5 COMPUTER ASSESSED

79 ORGANISATION

Overhead cost	Basis	Mending £	Stores £	Canteen £	Total £
Specific overheads	Allocate	4,000	1,000	2,000	7,000
Rent	Floor space	16,000	10,000	4,000	30,000
Building maintenance	Floor space	24,000	15,000	6,000	45,000
Machinery insurance	Value of machinery	1,344	1,056	0	2,400
Machinery depreciation	Value of machinery	6,160	4,840	0	11,000
Machinery running cost	Machinery hours	3,750	2,250	0	6,000
Power	Power usage	5,600	700	700	7,000
Total		60,854	34,846	12,700	108,400

80 ORGANISATION PART 2

Overhead cost	Basis	Mending £	Stores £	Canteen £	Total £
Sub-Total					
Re-apportion Canteen	Number of employees	9,525	3,175	-12,700	
Re-apportion Stores	Value of stores requisitions	38,021	-38,021		
Total		108,400			108,400

81   PACKAGING

	Original Budget	Flexed Budget	Actual	Variance
Volume sold	180,000	259,200	259,200	
	£000	£000	£000	£000
Sales revenue	3,600	3,600 ÷ 180 × 259.2 = 5,184	6,480	1,296
Less costs:				
Direct materials	630	630 ÷ 180 × 259.2 = 907	954	-47
Direct labour	720	720 ÷ 180 × 259.2 = 1,037	864	173
Overheads	1,764	(fixed) 1,764	2,210	-446
Operating profit	486	5,184 – (907 + 1,037 + 1,764) = 1,476	2,452	976

82   LF LTD

Task 1

	X	Y	Z
Total sales (£)	1,000,000	1,125,000	625,000
Total variable cost (£)	(750,000)	(750,000)	(500,000)
Total contribution (£)	250,000	375,000	125,000
Units sold	5,000	7,500	2,500
Contribution per unit	£50	£50	£50
Machine hours per unit	20	21	26
Contribution per machine hour	£2.50	£2.38	£1.92
Rank	1	2	3

Task 2

Production Plan

Product	Units	Hours used
X	5,000	100,000
Y	7,500	157,500
Z	39,000 ÷ 26 = 1,500	39,000
Total hours available		296,500

Task 3

Product	Units	Contribution per unit	Total contribution £
X	5,000	£50	250,000
Y	7,500	£50	375,000
Z	1,500	£50	75,000
			700,000
Fixed costs (200,000 + 315,000 + 130,000)			(645,000)
Total profit			55,000

83 HEATH

(a) $\dfrac{17,150}{19-12}=2,450\,\text{units}$

(b) $\dfrac{17,150}{7/19}=£46,550$

Or 2,450 × 19 = £46,550

(c)

Units of H sold	4,000	5,000
Margin of safety (units)	4,000 – 2,450 = 1,550 units	5,000 – 2,450 = 2,550 units
Margin of safety percentage	$\dfrac{4,000-2,450}{4,000}\times100=38.75\%$	$\dfrac{5,000-2,450}{5,000}\times100=51\%$

(d) $\dfrac{17,150+24,850}{7}=6,000\,\text{units}$

(e) The correct answer is **B** – an increase in selling price means that contribution per unit increases therefore fewer units have to be made to cover the fixed costs. If BEP is lower than the margin of safety is higher.

84   BLINDS

(a)   **Net present value**

	Year 0 £000	Year 1 £000	Year 2 £000	Year 3 £000
Capital expenditure	−547			
Sales income		290	340	400
Operating costs		−120	−120	−120
Net cash flows	−547	170	220	280
PV factors	1.0000	0.909	0.826	0.751
Discounted cash flows	−547	155	182	210
Net present value	0			

(b)   **Payback period**

Year	Cash flow £000	Cumulative cash flow £000
0	(547)	(547)
1	170	(377)
2	220	(157)
3	280	123

The payback period is **2** years and **7** months.

Months = 157/280 × 12 = 6.7 months.

(c)   **C** – given the NPV is zero, the IRR must be 10%.

(d)   If the NPV of a project is nil then the cost of capital equals the Internal Rate of Return (IRR).

True

(e)   If the IRR of an investment is higher than the company's cost of capital then the investment should go ahead.

True

85   FIFO AVCO

Characteristic	FIFO	AVCO
Potentially out of date valuation on issues.	✓	
The valuation of inventory rarely reflects the actual purchase price of the material.		✓
This inventory valuation method is particularly suited to inventory that consist of liquid materials e.g. oil.		✓
This inventory valuation method is particularly suited to inventory that has a short shelf life e.g. dairy products.	✓	
In times of rising prices this method will give higher profits.	✓	
In times of rising prices this method will give lower profits.		✓
Inventory is valued at the average of the cost of purchases.		✓
Inventory is valued at the most recent purchase cost.	✓	

86 DIRECT INDIRECT

Cost	Direct	Indirect
Basic pay for production workers	✓	
Supervisors wages		✓
Bonus for salesman		✓
Production workers overtime premium due to general pressures		✓
Holiday pay for production workers		✓
Sick pay for supervisors		✓
Time spent by production workers cleaning the machinery		✓

87 BONUS

(a)

	Units
Actual production	1,350,000
Standard production (4,830 hours at 200 units)	(966,000)
Excess production	384,000
Bonus %	$\dfrac{25\% \times 1,400,000}{4,000.000} = 8.75\%$ $\dfrac{10\% \times 384,000}{250,000} \times 100 = 15\%$
Group bonus rate per hour	0.15 × £20 = £3.00
Total group bonus	4,830 hours at £3.00 = £14,490

(b)

Basic pay 40 hours at £9.30 =	£372.00
Bonus pay 40 hours at £3.00 =	£120.00
Total pay	**£492.00**

88   HOLDINGS LTD

Description	Units	Unit cost £	Total cost £		Description	Units	Unit cost £	Total cost £
Input – components	300	11.25	3,375		Normal loss	30	5.00	150
Materials – coating			500		Output	290	49.35	14,312
Labour			5,760					
Overheads			3,840					
Abnormal gain	20	49.35	987					
	320		14,462			320		14,462

89   SILVER

Note: Using AVCO so the EU calculation will include all costs (including those b/f in OWIP) and all output, not just the work done this period.

Equivalent units		Material	Conversion
	Completed output	3,200	3,200
	Total EU	3,200	3,200
Costs	OWIP	53,800	42,000
	Period	135,000	98,800
	Total cost	188,800	140,800
Cost per EU		59	44

90   DEBIT OR CREDIT?

(a)   B

Indirect materials are overhead costs so debit production overhead. An issue of materials is a credit from the material control account

(b)   A

Direct labour costs are credited to wages and salaries and debited to work-in-progress.

(c)   D

Over-absorbed overheads increase profit, and so are recorded as a credit entry in the statement of profit and loss. The matching debit entry would be production overhead control account.

91 ANIMAL FEEDS

Marginal costing

	£000	£000
Sales		25,000
Opening inventory	0	
Production costs (3,780 + 8,820)	12,600	
Closing inventory (12,600/900×400)	5,600	
Cost of sales		7,000
Contribution		18,000
Fixed costs		2,805
Profit for the period		15,195

Absorption costing

	£000	£000
Sales		25,000
Opening inventory	0	
Production costs (3,780 + 8,820 + 1,800)	14,400	
Closing inventory (14,400/900×400)	6,400	
Cost of sales		8,000
Gross Profit		17,000
Non-production cost		1,005
Profit for the period		15,995

92 OAR

(a)   B

	£
Actual expenditure	56,389
Absorbed cost (12,400 × 1.02 × £4.25)	53,754
Total under-absorption	2,635

(b)   B

	£
Actual overhead	694,075
Under-absorbed overhead	(35,000)
Overhead absorbed	659,075

$$\text{OAR} = \frac{£659,075}{32,150} = £20.50$$

(c)   £14.00

	£
Actual overhead	138,000
Over-absorbed overhead	23,000
Therefore amount of overhead absorbed	161,000

Hours worked = 11,500.

Therefore, absorption rate per hour = £161,000/11,500 hours = £14 per hour.

TASK 6 HUMAN ASSESSED

93   HIGHLAND

Extended trial balance

Ledger account	Ledger balances		Adjustments	
	Dr £	Cr £	Dr £	Cr £
Accruals		1,330		300
Advertising	1,800			
Bank	17,912			
Capital		40,000		
Closing inventory			11,890	11,890
Depreciation charge				
Drawings	14,700			
Fixtures and fittings – accumulated depreciation		945		
Fixtures and fittings – cost	6,099			
Irrecoverable debts	345			
Allowance for doubtful debt adjustment				295
Electricity	1,587		300	
Loan		10,000		
Opening inventory	5,215			
Prepayment			12,500	
Allowance for doubtful debts		485	295	
Purchases	78,921			
Purchase returns				2,000
PLCA		14,000	2,400	
Rent	25,000			12,500
Revenue		145,825		
SLCA	9,500			
VAT control account		11,453		400
Wages	62,959			
	224,038	224,038	27,385	27,385

Key answer tips

(a)   SLCA 9,500 × 2% = 190. Allowance is currently £485, therefore put in an adjustment of (£485 - £190 =) £295 to reduce it to £190. Debit Allowance for doubtful debts £295, Credit Allowance for doubtful debts adjustment £295.

(c)   The prepayment for the year end is 10/12 × 15,000 = 12,500. For November and December X5 = 2/12 × 15,000 = 2,500. Total rental charge for the year = (10/12 × 12,000) + 2,500 = £12,500

(e)   Accrual for November and December. 2/3 × £450 = £300

94   ETB

Extended trial balance

Ledger account	Ledger balances		Adjustments		SoPL		SoFP	
	Dr £	**Cr £**	**Dr £**	**Cr £**	**Dr £**	**Cr £**	**Dr £**	**Cr £**
Accruals		2,300		425				2,725
Advertising	1,800				1,800			
Bank	7,912		1,175				9,087	
Capital		40,000						40,000
Closing inventory			6,590	6,590		6,590	6,590	
Depreciation charge			821		821			
Drawings	14,700						14,700	
Fixtures and fittings – accumulated depreciation		945		821				1,766
Fixtures and fittings – cost	6,099						6,099	
Interest	345				345			
Light and heat	1,587		706		2,293			
Loan		10,000						10,000
Opening inventory	5,215				5,215			
Prepayments	485		927	281			1,131	
Purchases	75,921				75,921			
PLCA		14,000						14,000
Rent and rates	38,000			927	37,073			
Revenue		145,825				145,825		
SLCA	9,500			1,175			8,325	
VAT control account		11,453						11,453
Wages	62,959				62,959			
Loss						34,012	34,012	
	224,523	224,523	10,219	10,219	186,427	186,427	79,944	79,944

95   VINCENT

Vincent Trading

Statement of financial position as at 30 June 20X8

	£	£	£
Non-current assets	Cost	Depreciation	Carrying amount
Equipment	17,500	4,500	13,000
Current assets			
Inventory		7,850	
Trade receivables (£7,800 – £840)		6,960	
Prepayments		3,200	
		18,010	
Current liabilities			
Payables (£6,800 + £1,450)	8,250		
VAT	2,950		
Accruals	750		
Bank	1,250		
		13,200	
Net current assets			4,810
Net assets			17,810
Financed by:			
Opening capital			17,000
Add: Net profit			8,810
Less: Drawings			8,000
Closing capital			17,810

96   BEALE

Beale – Statement of financial position as at 30 June 20X6			
	£	£	£
Non-current assets	Cost	Depreciation	Carrying amount
Motor vehicles	45,000	20,000	25,000
Current assets			
Inventory		17,500	
Trade receivables (£68,550 – £1,450)		67,100	
Cash		500	
		85,100	
Current liabilities			
Bank	2,250		
Trade payables	23,750		
Accruals	3,150		
VAT	3,500		
		32,650	
Net current assets			52,450
Net assets			77,450
Financed by:			
Opening capital			85,000
Less: Net loss			4,350
Less: Drawings			3,200
Closing capital			77,450

97   PEG

Partnership appropriation account for the year ended 30 June 20X9

	£
Profit for the year	220,000
Salaries:	
Gertrude	−18,000
Eddie	0
Polonius	−36,000
Interest on capital:	
Gertrude	−2,000
Eddie	−2,000
Polonius	−2,000
Sales commission:	
Gertrude	−8,250
Eddie	−6,800
Polonius	−4,715
Profit available for distribution	140,235
Profit share:	
Gertrude(40% × £140,235)	56,094
Ed (40% × £140,235)	56,094
Polonius (20% × £140,235)	28,047
Total residual profit distributed	140,235

98   CG

(a)

Account name	Dr	Cr
Goodwill	£105,000	
Capital account – Cordelia		£36,750
Capital account – Goneril		£68,250

(b)   £31,750

New goodwill value   = £105,000 + £22,000

= £127,000

× 25%   = £31,750

99   SHAKE A SPEAR

Capital account – Will

Bank	31,000	Balance b/d	9,000
		Goodwill	15,000
		Current account	7,000
	31,000		31,000

100   LEAF AND PETAL

	Leaf £	Petal £	Total £
Salaries	12,000	–	12,000
Interest on Capital	600	900	1,500
Interest on Drawings	(255)	(150)	(405)
Profit share ratio 3:2	32,343	21,562	53,905 (ß)
Total profit share	44,688	22,312	
Net profit from profit and loss account			67,000

Capital Account

	Leaf £	Petal £		Leaf £	Petal £
			Balance b/d	10,000	15,000
Balance c/d	10,000	15,000			
	10,000	15,000		10,000	15,000
			Balance b/d	10,000	15,000

Current Account

	Leaf £	Petal £		Leaf £	Petal £
Balance b/d		3,200	Balance b/d	7,700	
Drawings	12,000	10,000	Profit Share	44,688	22,312
Balance c/d	40,388	9,112			
	52,388	22,312		52,388	22,312
			Balance b/d	40,388	9,112

Section 3

MOCK ASSESSMENT – QUESTIONS

TASK 1 (15 MARKS)

This task is based on a workplace scenario separate to the rest of the assessment.

An accountant, Siobahn, has recently started work at Plug Ltd, a large organisation with many employees. She mainly works in the accounts department and is currently responsible for performing bank reconciliations and control account reconciliations. She is trying to apply the ethical code's conceptual framework to some ethical problems she is facing at work and is currently evaluating threats to her fundamental principles.

(a)   **Are these statements true or false?** (2 marks)

Statement	True	False
The AAT code of ethics gives detailed rules that cover a wide range of possible scenarios.		
Some of the ethical principles can be overlooked if it is in the public interest to do so.		

(b)   **For each of the following scenarios identify the nature of the ethical threat.** (2 marks)

Scenario	Threat
Siobahn is seconded to internal audit and asked to verify that control procedures have been followed correctly, including bank reconciliations.	
Siobahn's brother is one of Plug Ltd's suppliers.	

∇ Drop down list for task (b)

Self-interest threat
Self-review threat
Advocacy threat
Familiarity threat
Intimidation threat

An ex-boyfriend of Siobahn is demanding that she reveal confidential information about Plug Ltd's manufacturing processes or he will publish compromising photographs of her online.

(c) **Identify whether the following statements are true or false.** **(3 marks)**

Statement	True	False
Siobahn may never disclose confidential information to any third party.		
The threat that Siobahn is facing to her compliance with the fundamental principles is a self-interest threat.		
Siobahn must resign immediately from Plug Ltd as her integrity has been compromised by her past relationships.		

Terry is also an accountant as Plug Ltd and often helps the sales department when pitching for new contracts. Whilst pitching for a contract in the local area, Plug Ltd was competing against the main rival local firm. The competitor firm is in serious financial difficulties and approached Terry to offer him an all-expenses paid holiday in return for offering a more expensive price to the potential client. It turns out that the competitor would have gone into administration without this contract win. James has been unsure as to whether he should accept the offer.

(d) **Complete the following statement.** **(2 marks)**

Being offered gifts by the rival firm is ⌄ to Terry's fundamental

principle of ⌄

⌄ Drop down list for task (d)

a self-interest threat
a familiarity threat
objectivity
professional competence

Terry has decided not to accept the holiday and inflate his recommended price, despite his belief that Plug Ltd was unlikely to win the tender anyway.

(e) **Identify whether the following statements are true or false.** **(3 marks)**

Statement	True	False
Had he accepted the holiday, Terry would have been guilty of the offence of 'active' bribery under the UK Bribery Act (2010).		
The UK Bribery Act (2010) only applies to UK citizens, residents and companies established under UK law.		
Not all gifts or hospitality would be considered to be bribes.		

Recently Bath plc, a customer of Plug Ltd, sent in a cheque for £80,000 in payment of an invoice for £8,000. When Terry queried this, the client said it was a mistake and asked for a cheque for the difference of £72,000 to be written to Faucet plc, a sister company of Bath plc.

(f) **Identify whether the following statements are true or false.** **(3 marks)**

Statement	True	False
Terry should report the matter to the firm's MRLO.		
Plug Ltd should scrutinise the request carefully before agreeing to any payment.		
Unless investigations satisfy any concerns raised, then the MRLO should fill in a Suspicious Activity Report (SAR) to be sent to the NCA.		

TASK 2 (12 marks)

This task is based on the workplace scenario of Ovey and Sach.

You are Sam Jeffrey, a part-qualified Accounting Technician. You work for Ovey and Sach, a business which makes and sells designer gifts. Ovey and Sach is a partnership owned by Michelle Ovey and Andrew Sach.

You cover all aspects of bookkeeping and accounting for the business. Other accountants working at Ovey and Sach are Graham Hyde, another part-qualified technician and Susan Wright, the chief accountant.

You are checking the non-current assets register and some new fixtures and fittings for one of the shops has been added. You have located the purchase documentation.

The date is 30 March 20X6. Purchase details are as follows:

INVOICE	
Invoice to: Ovey and Sach Field Farm Shop Winstead M16 4PT Deliver to: Above address Delivery date: 28/03/X6	**Anderson Fittings** Westlife Park Gripton M7 1ZK Tel: 0161 439 2020 Fax: 0161 439 2121 Invoice no: 06447 Tax point: 10 March 20X6 VAT reg no: 432 1679 28 GB

Code	Description	Quantity	VAT rate	Unit price	Amount ex-VAT
			%	£	£
SU417	Shelving unit	2	20	50.00	100.00
GC254	Glass cabinet	3	20	75.00	225.00
					325.00
VAT					65.00
Total amount payable					390.00

Ovey and Sach are VAT registered and the VAT on this invoice has been recorded correctly in the accounts. The purchase was entered in the ledger accounts as:

Account	Debit	Credit
Purchases	325.00	
VAT	65.00	
Bank		390.00

(a)   **Complete the table below to show the journal to correct the treatment of this invoice**

(2 marks)

Account	Debit	Credit
Purchases/Bank/Fixtures and fittings		
Purchases/Bank/Fixtures and fittings		

(b)   **Complete the following sentence:**   **(1 mark)**

The journal will increase/decrease/cause no difference to Ovey and Sachs profit

You have been asked to prepare monthly management accounting information which includes detailed performance data that is used to calculate staff bonuses. Based on information you prepare this year's bonuses will be lower than expected.

You have had approached by colleagues offering various incentives to make accruals for additional revenue and other reversible adjustments, to enable all staff (including yourself) to receive increased or higher bonuses.

(c)   **Which TWO of following ethical principles do you face?**   **(2 marks)**

Integrity	
Confidentiality	
Professional competence and due care	
Objectivity	
Professional behaviour	

(d)   **Which ONE of following ethical threats do you face?**   **(1 marks)**

Advocacy threat	
Self-review threat	
Intimidation threat	
Self-interest threat	

It is now 14 October. You have just received an invoice from Briggs Ltd where the VAT has been incorrectly calculated. You rang the supplier to query this and were told that your colleague, Graham Hyde, was aware of this and always agreed to the invoices before.

You suspect that your colleague is involved in fraud and possibly even money laundering but are not sure what best to do next.

(e)   Which of the following options describes what you should do next?   **(2 marks)**

Confront Graham with your suspicions	
Discuss the matter with Susan Wright, the chief accountant	
Call the police	
Resign	

Michelle Ovey and Andrew Sach are worried whether there are other issues relating to the recording of purchases and amounts owed to suppliers. As a result of this, they ask you to perform a logic check of purchase ledger transactions for the month of September 20X6.

The Purchase ledger control account balance at 1 September was £14,875. You have verified the following figures as much as possible, by confirming balances with suppliers, with which you construct the following purchase ledger control account

(f)   'Drag and drop' the option below to construct the purchase ledger control account for the month of September 20X6   **(2 marks)**

Balance b/d	14,875
Cash book	2,365
Purchase day book	4,256
Contra	100
Balance c/d	15,977

Purchases ledger control account

	£		£

(g)   Calculate the missing figure in the purchases ledger control account.   **(1 mark)**

£	

(h)   Which of the following could the missing figure represent?   **(1 marks)**

Overstated purchase invoices	
Understated purchase invoices	

TASK 3 (13 marks)

This task is based on the workplace scenario of Ovey and Sach.

Today's date is 31 January 20X7.

Ovey and Sach are introducing a new product, the DFG. The budget is to sell 1,200 units 20X7 at an average selling price of £14. Incremental fixed production costs were budgeted to be £6,000 and the average variable production cost was expected to be £6 per unit.

(a) **Using the information above, determine the following budgeted figures for DFG for the year to 31 December 20X7, to the nearest whole number.** (3 marks)

    (i)   Breakeven sales volume (units)

    (ii)   Total breakeven contribution (£)

    (iii) Margin of safety (units)

Michelle amended the budget as follows:

- 1,200 units to be made but only 1,100 units to be sold.

- The average variable production cost will be £6.50 per unit.

- The average selling price will be £13.45 per unit.

- Total fixed production costs will be £6,240.

(b) **Calculate the profit figures for the year to 31 December 20X7 under the following scenarios.** (2 marks)

    (i)   Profit if inventory is valued at marginal cost (£)

    (ii)   Profit if inventory is valued at full cost (£)

(c) **Explain the difference in profit between using marginal and absorption costing to value inventory.** (4 marks)

Ovey and Sach have a policy for accruals and prepayments as follows - an entry is made into the income or expense account and an opposite entry into the relevant asset or liability account. In the following period the entry is reversed.

You are looking at rental expenses for the year ended 31 March 20X8.

The cash book for the year shows payments for rent of £10,550.

This includes payments for two properties. Rental for the period:

Property A: 1 January to 31 December 20X8 £1,500

Property B: 1 April 20X8 to 31 March 20X9 £2,900

(d) **Calculate the value of the adjustment required for rental expenses as at 31 March 20X8.**

£

(2 marks)

(e) **Update the rental expenses account.** **(2 marks)**

You must show:

- the cash book figure

- the year-end adjustment

- the transfer to the statement or profit or loss for the year.

Rental expenses

Prepaid expenses (reversal)	1,800		

TASK 4 **(15 marks)**

This task is based on the workplace scenario of Ovey and Sach.

Today's date is 31 March 20X8.

Michelle Ovey and Andrew Sach have decided to raise additional finance to increase the product range and grow the business. As part of a loan application they need to produce a report for the bank. Unfortunately, Susan Wright is currently off sick and Andrew Sach has told you to produce the report.

The deadline suggested appears unrealistic, especially given the complexity of the work.

You feel that you are not sufficiently experienced to complete the work alone but your manager appears unable to offer the necessary support. You feel slightly intimidated by Andrew Sachs, and also feel under pressure to be a 'team player' and help out. However, if you try to complete the work to the required quality but fail, you could be subject to criticism and other repercussions.

(a) **Explain TWO threats to your ethical principles from Andrew Sach's request, and explain what actions you should take next. In your answer you should refer to the guidance found in the ethical code for professional accountants.** **(5 marks)**

Threat 1

Threat 2

Actions I should take

You receive the following email from Andrew Sach:

To: Sam Jeffrey

From: Andrew Sach

Date: 5/4/X8

Hello Sam

We have decided to delay completing the loan application until Susan is back with us as we feel it is vital that we get this right. Obviously we would still appreciate your input but want Susan to check everything before it goes to the bank.

In preliminary discussions with the bank I got the distinct impression that they would consider our application more favourably if we became a limited company rather than remain the partnership we currently operate as. I must confess to being confused and am now wondering whether we should be trying to raise new equity finance.

I would like you to tell me more about the implications of a partnership becoming a limited company as far as finance is concerned.

Please include three sections in your response to me as follows:

1   A brief description of a limited company and how switching could change the liability faced by Michelle Ovey and myself.

2   Three reasons why the bank may prefer to lend to companies rather than partnerships.

3   The difference in the way companies can raise equity finance compared to a partnership.

Regards,
Andrew

(b)   Reply to Andrew, addressing all three points that he has raised.   **(10 marks)**

To:	Andrew Sachs
From:	Sam Jeffrey
Date:	5/4/X8

Subject:	
1	
2	

TASK 5 (12 marks)

This task is based on the workplace scenario of Ovey and Sach.

Michelle Sach has provided you with the following information to produce an alternative scenario for the budget.

- Material and labour costs are variable

- There is an allowance for an energy rise of 10.0% already in the first draft. Revise the energy price rise to 8.0%

- Increase the selling price by 5.0%

- Reduce the sales volume by 8.0%

(a) **Complete the second draft column in the operating budget table** **(4 marks)**

For the sales price per unit figure, enter two decimal places, if relevant. For the other figures, round to the nearest whole number, if necessary.

Operating budget	First draft	Second draft
Sales price per unit (£)	15.00	
Sales volume	75,000	
		£
Sales revenue	1,125,000	
Costs		
Material	131,250	
Labour	187,500	
Energy	44,000	
Depreciation	62,400	56,160
Total	425,150	
Gross Profit	699,850	

Michelle has asked you to analyse the overheads for two products - Design products and Own products. Both product lines absorb their overheads based on machine hours.

Design products has budgeted overheads of £5,997,232 while Own products has budgeted overheads of £2,844,968.

The budgeted number of machine hours for Quarter 1 are:

Branded products   187,414

Own label products   118,540

(b) **Calculate the overhead absorption rates for both products (to the nearest whole pound).**

(2 mark)

	Design products	**Own products**
Rate per machine hour		

Assume that at the end of Quarter 1 the actual overheads incurred in the Branded products profit centre were £1,506,000, and the actual machine hours operated were 48,000 hours.

(c) **Calculate the under or over absorption for Quarter 1.** **(3 marks)**

		£
Overhead absorbed		
Overhead incurred		
Absorption	OVER/UNDER (Delete as appropriate.)	

(d) **Complete the following table to show the journal entries for the absorption of overheads in Quarter 1.** **(3 marks)**

	Debit (£)	**Credit (£)**
Overhead absorbed		
Under/over absorption		
Overhead control account		

TASK 6 (13 marks)

This task is based on the workplace scenario of Ovey and Sach.

You have been provided with a partially completed extended trial balance for the year ended 31/12/X8. The person who was working on it has left the company and you have been asked to complete it.

(a) **Extend the entries, where necessary, into the appropriate Statement of profit or loss or Statement of financial position columns in the extended trial balance below.** **(5 marks)**

(b) A profit of £2,968 has been calculated correctly. Enter this figure in the relevant places in the extended trial balance below. **(2 marks)**

Account name	Trial balance		Adjustments		Statement of profit or loss		Statement of fin. pos.	
	Dr £	Cr £	Dr £	Cr £	Dr £	Cr £	Dr £	Cr £
Capital		7,830						7,830
Cash	2,010						2,010	
NCA cost	9,420						9,420	
Accumulated depreciation		3,470		942				4,412
SLCA	1,830						1,830	
Opening inventory	1,680				1,680			
PLCA		390						390
Revenue		14,420				14,420		
*Purchases	8,180			1,500				
*Rent	1,100		100					
Electricity	940		400		1,340			
*Rates	950			200				
Depreciation charges			942		942			
Drawings			1,500				1,500	
Accruals				500				500
*Prepayments			200					
*Closing inventory			1,140	1,140				
*Profit								

The following day Michelle noticed that there is no allowance for doubtful debts in the accounts yet so this will need to be set up. The amount of the allowance is 3% of receivables needs to be added.

(c) Complete the journal (including the narrative) to include the adjustment. Calculate the adjustment to the nearest whole pound. **(5 marks)**

Date	Account	Debit £	Credit £
31/12/X8			
31/12/X8			
Narrative			

(d) Calculate the revised profit or loss for the year ended 31/12/X8. Use a minus sign to indicate a loss. **(1 marks)**

£

Section 4

MOCK ASSESSMENT – ANSWERS

TASK 1   **(15 marks)**

(a)   **Are these statements true or false?**   **(2 marks)**

Statement	True	False
The AAT code of ethics gives detailed rules that cover a wide range of possible scenarios.		x
Some of the ethical principles can be overlooked if it is in the public interest to do so.	x	

Note:

1   The code gives principles rather than rules.

2   An example of this would be whistleblowing, where confidentiality is breached.

(b)   **For each of the following scenarios identify the nature of the ethical threat.**   **(2 marks)**

Scenario	Threat
Siobahn is seconded to internal audit and asked to verify that control procedures have been followed correctly, including bank reconciliations.	Self-review threat
Siobahn's brother is one of Plug Ltd's suppliers.	Familiarity threat

(c)   **Identify whether the following statements are true or false.**   **(3 marks)**

Statement	True	False
Siobahn may never disclose confidential information to any third party.		x
The threat that Siobahn is facing to her compliance with the fundamental principles is a self-interest threat.		x
Siobahn must resign immediately from Plug Ltd as her integrity has been compromised by her past relationships.		x

Note:

1   Siobahn may disclose information if given permission to do so.

2   This is an example of an intimidation threat.

3   Siobahn should discuss the matter with her manager and possibly even with the police.

(d) **Complete the following statement.** (2 marks)

Being offered gifts by the rival firm is | a self-interest threat | to Terry's fundamental principle of | objectivity |

(e) **Identify whether the following statements are true or false.** (3 marks)

Statement	True	False
Had he accepted the holiday, Terry would have been guilty of the offence of 'active' bribery under the UK Bribery Act (2010).		x
The UK Bribery Act (2010) only applies to UK citizens, residents and companies established under UK law.		x
Not all gifts or hospitality would be considered to be bribes.	x	

Note:

1   Terry would have been guilty of "passive" bribery – receiving a bribe.

2   The UK Act also applies to.

3   Very small gifts or acts of hospitality would not be considered bribes.

(f) **Identify whether the following statements are true or false.** (3 marks)

Statement	True	False
Terry should report the matter to the firm's MRLO.	x	
Plug Ltd should scrutinise the request carefully before agreeing to any payment.	x	
Unless investigations satisfy any concerns raised, then the MRLO should fill in a Suspicious Activity Report (SAR) to be sent to the NCA.	x	

Note:

There is a strong suspicion of money laundering in these circumstances.

TASK 2 (12 marks)

(a) Complete the table below to show the journal to correct the treatment of this invoice.

(2 marks)

Account	Debit	Credit
Purchases		325
Fixtures and fittings	325	

(b) Complete the following sentence: (1 mark)

The journal will **increase** Ovey and Sachs profit.

(c) Which TWO of following ethical principles do you face? (2 marks)

Integrity	x
Confidentiality	
Professional competence and due care	
Objectivity	x
Professional behaviour	

(d) Which ONE of following ethical threats do you face? (1 marks)

Advocacy threat	
Self-review threat	
Intimidation threat	
Self-interest threat	x

(e) Which of the following options describes what you should do next? (2 marks)

Confront Graham with your suspicions	
Discuss the matter with Susan Wright, the chief accountant	x
Call the police	
Resign	

(f) 'Drag and drop' the option below to construct the purchase ledger control account for the month of September 20X6. (2 marks)

Purchases ledger control account

	£		£
		Balance b/d	14,875
		Purchases day book	4,256
Contra	100		
Cash book	2,365		
Balance c/d	15,977		

(g) Calculate the missing figure in the purchases ledger control account. (1 mark)

£	689

(h) Which of the following could the missing figure represent? (2 marks)

Overstated purchase invoices	x
Understated purchase invoices	

Given the difference is on the debit side, then one cause could be the credit side being too high – the PDB figure is overstated.

TASK 3   (13 marks)

(a) Determine the following budgeted figures for DFG for the year to 31 December 20X7, to the nearest whole number. (3 marks)

(i)	Breakeven sales volume	750
(ii)	Total breakeven contribution	6,000
(iv)	Margin of safety	450

(b) Calculate the profit for the year to 31 December 20X7 under the following scenarios. (2 marks)

(iii)	Profit if inventory is valued at marginal cost (£)	1,405
(iv)	Profit if inventory is valued at full cost (£)	1,925

	Marginal Costing	Absorption costing
	£	£
Revenue (1,200×£13.45)	14,795	14,795
Cost of sales		
Opening inventory	0	0
Production	1,200×6.50=7,800	(1,200×6.50)+6,240=14,040
Less: Closing inventory	7,800/1,200×100=650	14,040/1,200×100=1,170
	7,150	12,870
Contribution or Gross Profit	7,645	1,925
Less: Fixed costs	6,240	0
Profit	1,405	1,925

(c)   Closing inventory is valued at £1,170 under absorption costing and £650 under marginal costing. The absorption costing valuation is £520 higher due to fixed production overheads being absorbed.

This £520 higher valuation has resulted in profit being £520 higher under absorption costing (£1,925) compared to marginal costing (£1,405).

(d)   £4,025 (Calculated as: (9/12 × £1,500) + £2,900)

(e)   **Rental expenses**

Prepaid expenses (reversal)	1,800	Prepaid expenses	4,025
Bank	10,550	Statement of profit or loss	8,325
	_____		_____
	12,350		12,350
	_____		_____

TASK 4   (15 marks)

(a)   **Threat 1**   (5 marks)

> **Professional competence and due care:**
>
> It would not be right for me to attempt to complete work that is technically beyond my abilities without proper supervision.
>
> This is made worse by my concern whether it is even possible to complete the work within the time available and still act diligently to achieve the required quality of output.

Threat 2

> **Objectivity:**
>
> Pressure from Andrew Sach, combined with the fear of repercussions, gives rise to an intimidation threat to my objectivity.
>
> If the loan application is unsuccessful then there is also the possibility that will impact other people's jobs, again adding to threat to objectivity.

Actions I should take

> I should use the Conceptual Framework to apply relevant safeguards to bring the threat to ethical principles down to an acceptable level OR I should use the ethical conflict resolution process stated in the code. I should follow any internal procedure for reporting/dealing with such threats.
>
> I should discuss my concerns with Andrew Sachs that I do not have sufficient time and experience to complete the work to a satisfactory standard and suggest how the problem may be resolved. For example, the use of a subcontract accountant or the possibility of assigning another member of staff to supervise my work.
>
> If I am still under pressure to do the work, then I should get advice from the AAT and as to what to do next.
>
> It would be unethical to attempt to complete the work if I doubt my competence.

(b) **Reply to Andrew, addressing all three points that he has raised.** **(10 marks)**

To:	Andrew Sachs
From:	Sam Jeffrey
Date:	5/4/X8

Subject:	Raising finance

1

Limited companies

A limited company is an organisation that is a separate legal entity distinct from its owners (unlike a partnership or sole trader). The ownership of a company is through share ownership.

At present Michelle Ovey and yourself have unlimited personal liability for partnership debts. With a "limited" company the liability of owners (shareholders) is limited to any unpaid amounts on shares purchased. Thus, for example, the bank would not be able to pursue Michelle Ovey and yourself if the business struggled to repay the loan.

For this reason, some banks may insist on personal guarantees from the owners, separate from the company.

2

Bank loans

Banks may prefer to lend to companies for the following reasons:

1   A limited company must prepare annual accounts (also known as 'statutory accounts') from the company's records at the end of the financial year. Partners are not legally required to produce annual accounts or file accounts for inspection.

2   Larger companies' financial statements must be audited, possibly making them more reliable and accurate.

3 A company's   accounts must be prepared in accordance with the Companies Act 2006, possibly making it easier to assess the business' performance

3

Equity finance

Companies can raise equity finance by issuing new shares to investors.

With partnerships, either the existing partners could introduce further capital or a new partner could be admitted. Introducing new partners would involve having to change the partnership agreement.

TASK 5 (12 marks)

(a) (4 marks)

Operating budget	First draft	Alternative scenario
Sales price per unit (£)	15.00	
Sales volume	75,000	
		£
Sales revenue	1,125,000	1,086,750
Costs		
Material	131,250	120,750
Labour	187,500	172,500
Energy	44,000	43,200
Depreciation	62,400	56,160
Total	425,150	392,610
Gross Profit	699,850	694,140

Workings

Selling price increase = £15.00 × 1.05 = £15.75.

Decrease in sales volume = 75,000 × 92% = 69,000 units.

Sales revenue = £15.75 × 69,000 = £1,086,750.

Material costs = £131,250/75,000 × 69,000 = £120,750.

Labour costs = £187,500/75,000 × 69,000 = £172,500.

Energy costs (remove 10% increase) = £44,000/90% = £40,000.

Energy cost increase of 8% = £40,000 × 1.08 = £43,200.

(b) (2 mark)

	Design products	Own products
Rate per machine hour	£5,997,232/187,414 = £32	£2,844,968/118,540 = £24

(c) (3 marks)

Overhead absorbed	48,000 hours at £32	£1,536,000
Overhead incurred		£1,506,000
Absorption	OVER	£30,000

(d) (3 marks)

	Debit (£)	Credit (£)
Overhead absorbed	1,536,000	
Over absorption		30,000
Overhead control account		1,506,000

TASK 6   **(13 MARKS)**

(a) and (b)   **(5 and 2 marks)**

Account name	Trial balance		Adjustments		Statement of profit or loss		Statement of fin. pos.	
	Dr £	Cr £	Dr £	Cr £	Dr £	Cr £	Dr £	Cr £
Capital		7,830						7,830
Cash	2,010						2,010	
NCA cost	9,420						9,420	
Accumulated depreciation		3,470		942				4,412
SLCA	1,830						1,830	
Opening inventory	1,680				1,680			
PLCA		390						390
Revenue		14,420				14,420		
Purchases	8,180			1,500	6,680			
Rent	1,100		100		1,200			
Electricity	940		400		1,340			
Rates	950			200	750			
Depreciation charges			942		942			
Drawings			1,500				1,500	
Accruals				500				500
Prepayments			200				200	
Closing inventory			1,140			1,140	1,140	
Profit					2,968			2,968

(c)   Complete the journal (including the narrative) to include the adjustment. Calculate the adjustment to the nearest whole pound.   **(5 marks)**

There is no allowance in the accounts yet so this will need to be set up. The amount of the allowance is 3% of receivables therefore £1,830 × 3% = £55

Date	Account	Debit £	Credit £
31/12/X8	Allowance for doubtful debt adjustment	55	
31/12/X8	Allowance for doubtful debts		55
Narrative	Being the creation of the allowance for doubtful debts for the year ended 31st December 20X8		

(d) Calculate the revised profit or loss for the year ended 31/12/X8. Use a minus sign to indicate a loss. **(1 marks)**

£2,913

The allowance for doubtful debts adjustment is an expense account to the statement of profit or loss debit column so this will reduce profit. £2,968 – 55 = £2,913

Section 5

SAMPLE ASSESSMENT – QUESTIONS

ASSESSMENT INFORMATION

You have **2 hours and 30 minutes** to complete this sample assessment.

- This assessment contains 6 tasks and you should attempt to complete every task.

- Each task is independent. You will not need to refer to your answers to previous tasks.

- The total number of marks for this assessment is 80.

- Read every task carefully to make sure you understand what is required.

- Task 3 and Task 4 require extended writing as part of your response to these questions. You should make sure you allow adequate time to complete these tasks.

- Where the date is relevant, it is given in the task data.

- Both minus signs and brackets can be used to indicate negative numbers unless task instructions state otherwise.

- You must use a full stop to indicate a decimal point. For example, write 100.57 not 100, 57 or 10057.

- You may use a comma to indicate a number in the thousands, but you don't have to. For example, 10000 and 10, 000 are both acceptable.

SCENARIO

Task 1 is based on a workplace scenario separate to the rest of the assessment

Task 2 to **Task 6** are based on the workplace scenario of BLM & Co.

You are a part-qualified accounting technician working for BLM & Co, a business which manufactures and sells sinks. BLM & Co is owned and run by Brian and Lakmani Moore in partnership.

You cover all aspects of bookkeeping and accounting for the business, along with Jed Malone, who is responsible in particular for completing the VAT return.

BLM & Co also uses the services of Addo & Co, a firm of accountants. Keira Jackson is the accountant at Addo & Co who carries out tasks for BLM & Co.

TASK 1 (15 MARKS)

Wajid is an accountant who works for Laleham Ltd, a large organisation with many employees.

Tara, a new accountant with Laleham Ltd, has made two statements to Wajid about how she believes the ethical code applies to her.

(a) **Identify whether the following statements are true or false.** (2 marks)

Statement	True	False
'I have no duty to act in the public interest provided that I act in the interests of Laleham Ltd and the accountancy profession.'		
'The ethical code provides detailed rules on how I should act in every possiblesituation that I might encounter at work.'		

(b) **Identify whether or not the ethical code specifically requires Tara to take each of the following actions in order to act in line with the principle of professional behaviour.**

(2 marks)

Action	Required	Not required
Comply with all regulations that affect Laleham Ltd.		
Promote the reputation of the profession at every opportunity.		

Wajid has noticed that Tara does not conduct her work thoroughly and she often completes it late. He believes that, as a result of Tara's lack of diligence, she is in breach of one of the fundamental principles.

(c) **Identify which fundamental principle Tara has breached.** (2 marks)

	✓
Integrity	
Professional competence and due care	
Objectivity	

Tara has been told that she is facing disciplinary procedures because she has behaved unethically.

(d) **Identify whether or not each organisation below may bring disciplinary procedures againstTara for her unethical behaviour.** (3 marks)

Organisation	May bring disciplinary procedures	May NOT bring disciplinary procedures
AAT		
The National Crime Agency (NCA)		
Laleham Ltd (Tara's employer)		

Employment regulations require employers to pay workers at least the National Minimum Wage (NMW).

Laleham Ltd makes high levels of profits. The Chief Executive insists that managers should be paid a veryhigh rate with regular bonuses, but workers should receive only NMW, with no entitlement to bonuses.

(e)   Identify whether the following statements are true or false.   **(2 marks)**

Statement	True	False
The Chief Executive's policy on employee pay raises doubts about the ethical nature of the leadership and culture of Laleham Ltd.		
Because Laleham Ltd complies with the NMW regulations, it is automatically considered to be behaving ethically in relation to its employees.		

Ian is an accountant who has just started working for Penton Ltd, reporting to Hettie, who is also an accountant. Ian has discovered a material error in Penton Ltd's last corporation tax return.

(f)   Identify the action Ian must now take.   **(2 marks)**

Action	✓
Resign	
Advise HMRC of the error without disclosing any information to Hettie or Penton Ltd	
Tell Hettie about the error and recommend that Penton Ltd disclose the error to HMRC	

Hettie realises that she has inadvertently become involved in Penton Ltd's money laundering operation.

(g)   Complete the following statement.   **(2 marks)**

Hettie may have a defence against a money laundering charge if she makes _____to the relevant authority.

Options
a protected disclosure
an authorised disclosure
a prompt disclosure

TASK 2   **(12 MARKS)**

Today's date is 15 January 20X8.

You are checking an invoice that was issued to a customer yesterday. The invoice is incomplete

From: **BLM & Co** **200 -210 Farm Road** **Endsleigh** **EN61 7DS**	To: **Emporium Ltd** **178 Judd Road** **Endsleigh** **EN62 8SP**	Invoice date: **14 January 20X8**	Invoice number: **CJL69840**
Purchase Order: 3214	Deliver date: 27/12/X7		
Description	**Quantity**	**Per unit** **£**	**£**
Jade 1.5 bowl and drainer	15 units	145.00	2,175.00
		VAT at 20%	0.00
		Total	2,175.00

(a)   **Calculate the VAT amount for this invoice and the new invoice total.**   **(2 marks)**

VAT to include on this invoice: £	
Invoice total including VAT: £	

(b)   **Identify what the impact on BLM's profit for the year is, if the invoice error is not corrected.**   **(1 mark)**

	✓
BLM's profit will be higher.	
BLM's profit will be lower.	
BLM's profit will not change.	

Jed Malone, your fully qualified colleague, has refused to change the invoice as he doesn't want to upset the customer by increasing the invoice amount.

(c)   **Identify what your next action should be.**   **(1 mark)**

	✓
Send a Suspicious Activity Report to the National Crime Agency.	
Tell Brian and Lakmani about your concerns.	

You discover that BLM & Co has been supplying sinks to Malone Ltd, a company owned and run by the brother of your fully-qualified colleague, Jed Malone. When you look at the relevant invoices, you realise that Jed has been overstating sales and misrecording VAT. As a result, Malone Ltd qualifies for a 15% trade discount on its future purchases from BLM & Co.

(d) **Applying the conceptual framework from the ethical code, complete the sentence below todescribe the situation faced by Jed when recording sales to his brother's company.** **(2 marks)**

_____GAP 1_____threat to_____GAP 2_____.

Gap 1 Options	✓	Gap 2 Options	✓
A self-review…		objectivity.	
A familiarity…		professional competence and due care.	
An intimation…		professional behaviour.	

You conclude that the deliberate misrecording of VAT is unethical behaviour by Jed.

(e) **Identify what your next action should be.** **(1 mark)**

	✓
Notify HMRC of the VAT error.	
Tell Brian and Lakmani about your concerns.	

On the morning of 16 January, Jed is dismissed for misconduct by BLM & Co and leaves the office. You aretemporarily BLM & Co's only member of the finance team. A VAT officer will be coming to the office for a planned visit on the afternoon of 16 January. You are not prepared for this visit and do not believe you can answer any questions from the VAT officer effectively. Brian and Lakmani insist that you must be present and deal with the VAT officer without assistance.

You feel intimidated by Brian and Lakmani's insistence that you must be present to deal with the VAT officerunassisted.

(f) **Identify what your next action should be.** **(1 mark)**

	✓
Resign from BLM & Co.	
Seek external advice from AAT.	
Agree to deal with the VAT officer in line with your employers' instructions.	

Because of Jed's misconduct, Brian and Lakmani have asked you to examine his recording of sales ledgertransactions for the three months ended 31 December 20X7. You identify the following information:

Sales ledger control account balance at 1 October 20X7: £492,409

From 1 October to 31 December:

- Receipts from credit customers: £934,076

- Sales to credit customers, including VAT: £970,370

- Returns from credit customers, including VAT: £21,177

- Irrecoverable debts written off, including VAT: £4,330.

Amounts owed at 31 December 20X7, as confirmed by credit customers: £487,354.

(g) Drag each of the four options below to the appropriate column to reconstruct the sales ledgercontrol account for the three months ended 31 December 20X7. **(2 marks)**

Sales ledger control account

Balance b/d	492,409		
		Balance c/d	487,354

Options:

Cash book	934,076
Sales day book	970,370
Sales returns day book	21,177
Journal (irrecoverable debt)	4,330

(h) Calculate the missing figure in the sales ledger control account. **(1 mark)**

£

(i) Identify which of the following the missing figure could represent. **(1 mark)**

	✓
Discounts allowed.	
Direct debit from customer returned unpaid by the bank.	
Cash sales.	

TASK 3 **(13 marks)**

Today's date is 31 January 20X8.

From the cost accounting records, you can see that on 1 January 20X8, BLM & Co had 8,000 kg of raw material inventory. The cost recorded was £18,000. In January 20X8, the following movements took place:

6 Jan: 1,600 kg purchased for £3,440

11 Jan: 3,200 kg purchased for £7,360

13 Jan: 9,200 kg issued to production

The partners want to know how the remaining inventory of 3,600 kg would be valued using the FIFO methodof cost accounting.

(a) Using the FIFO method, value the inventory held on 31 January. **(2 marks)**

£

(b) **Identify which of the following is the correct journal for recording the year-end inventory.**

(1 mark)

	✓
DEBIT Purchases, CREDIT Closing inventory (current asset)	
DEBIT Closing inventory (current asset), CREDIT Purchases	
DEBIT Closing inventory (current asset), CREDIT Closing inventory (cost of sales)	
DEBIT Closing inventory (cost of sales), CREDIT Closing inventory (current asset)	

BLM & Co manufactures jade sinks in batches of 20. In the last production run in 20X7, the following costs were incurred for the batch:

	£
Direct materials	1,020
Direct labour	960
Prime cost	**1,980**
Variable production overheads	240
Fixed production overheads	280
Fixed non-production overheads	100
Total costs	**2,600**

At 31 December 20X7, three jade sinks were held in inventory. BLM & Co usually values inventory at full absorption cost.

(c) **(i)** **Explain how inventory of unsold sinks is valued differently depending on whether marginal or full absorption cost is used. You must show your workings.** **(4 marks)**

(ii) **Explain the effect of using the two different methods mentioned in (i) on the partnership's reported profit. You must show your workings.** **(2 marks)**

As at 31 December 20X7, BLM & Co's closing inventory valuation was £36,800. The partners expect to make sales of £3,190,000 in 20X8, and they expect the inventory valuation to rise by 10% by the year end. The gross margin is expected to be 45%, after deducting direct materials and direct labour.

(d) **Calculate how much BLM & Co expect to spend on direct materials and labour in 20X8. You must show your workings.** **(4 marks)**

TASK 4 (15 marks)

Today's date is 28 February 20X8.

Brian has asked you to prepare some financial statements urgently. These include a statement of cash flowsand a cash budget. He needs to send these to the bank by the end of the week as part of a loan application. Brian tells you that obtaining the loan is very important for the survival of the business. The jobs of everyonein the business depend on this. You have not yet studied statements of cash flows or cash budgets.

(a)   (i)   Identify TWO threats to your ethical principles as a result of Brian's request

(2 marks)

(ii)   State what response you should give to Brian in order to remain ethical.   (1 mark)

(iii)   State ONE reason for your response to Brian.   (1 mark)

Your role at BLM & Co includes:

- supporting sustainability throughout the business

- measuring sustainability in the business.

(b) **State why you, as an accountant, have a professional duty to uphold sustainability in your work.** **(1 mark)**

You receive the following email from Lakmani Moore:

To: Sam Jones <Sam.Jones@BLMCo.co.uk>
From: Lakmani Moore <Lakmani.Moore@BLMCO.co.uk>
Date: 28/2/X8
Subject: BLM & CO: change in structure
Good morning Sam, Brian and I are considering operating the business as a limited company. I would like you to tell me more about the implications of a partnership becoming a limited company. Please include three sections in your response to me as follows: 1   A brief description of a limited company 2   A summary of our position as owners if the business becomes a limited company 3   Explanation of one key advantage and one key disadvantage of operating as a limited company Regards, Lakmani

(c)   **Write an email to Lakmani, addressing all points that have been raised.**   **(10 marks)**

TASK 5 (12 marks)

BLM & Co has two profit centres, Retail and Manufacturing, and one support cost centre, Administration. Administration supports the two profit centres with 70% of its time spent with Retail and 30% of its time withManufacturing.

The budgeted overheads for the quarter ended 31 March 20X8 are shown below. You have been asked tohelp with the allocation and apportionment of the overheads.

Budgeted overheads	£	£
Depreciation		153,725
Rent and rates		130,000
Salaries		354,750
Retail	98,900	
Manufacturing	137,600	
Administration	118,250	
Total		638,475

The following information is also available:

Department	Carrying amount of machinery £	Power usage kWh	Floor space Sq M
Retail	19,500	22,000	750
Manufacturing	195,000	198,000	1,250
Administration	0	0	1,000
Total	214,500	220,000	3,000

(a) Complete the following overhead apportionment table. Show your answers to the nearest whole pound. Use minus signs where appropriate. (6 marks)

Overhead apportionment table

(Note: in the computerised version the totals would calculate automatically)

Budgeted overheads	Basis of apportionment	Retail	Manufacturing	Administration	Total
Depreciation	OPTION 1			0	AUTOSUM
Rent and rates	Floor Space	32,500	54,167	43,333	130,000
Salaries	Allocated	98,900	137,600	118,250	354,750
		AUTOSUM	AUTOSUM	AUTOSUM	AUTOSUM
Reapportion administration					
Total		AUTOSUM	AUTOSUM		AUTOSUM

Options:
Administration
Carrying amount of machinery
Depreciation
Floor space
Machinery at cost
Power usage

You have been asked to flex the original budget based on actual activity.

(b) **Complete the following table. Show your answers to the nearest whole pound.Adverse variances must be denoted with a minus sign or brackets.** **(6 marks)**

	Original budget £ 5,000 units	Flexed budget £	Actual results £ 6,000 units	Variance £
Sales revenue	1,240,000		1,500,000	
Variable costs	597,000		705,200	
Fixed overheads	638,475		638,875	
Operating profit	4,525		155,925	

TASK 6 (13 marks)

Note: This task is human marked. Students will be required to make text and numeric entries in both thepartnership appropriation statement and the current account.

You are preparing the final accounts for BLM & Co for the year ended 31 December 20X7. The statement ofprofit or loss for BLM & Co shows a profit for the year ended 31 December 20X7 of £247,982.

For the year ended 31 December 20X7, in accordance with the partnership agreement:

- Lakmani is entitled to a salary of £25,000 per year

- interest on capital has been calculated as £4,350 for Brian and £2,850 for Lakmani

- Brian has taken drawings of £91,200 over the year, and Lakmani has taken drawings of £84,400

- interest on drawings has been calculated at £300 for Brian and £180 for Lakmani for the year

- the residual profit after adjustments is shared between Brian and Lakmani in the ratio 3:2.

(a) **Complete the partnership appropriation account in accordance with the partnership agreement for the year ended 31 December 20X7. Show your answers as positive and to the nearest whole pound. There does not need to be an entry in every space.** **(7 marks)**

Partnership appropriation statement for year ended 31 December 20X7

	Total	Brian	Lakmani
Profit for the year			
Add			
Total	AUTOSUM		
Less appropriation of profits			
Total	AUTOSUM		
Profit available for distribution			
Profit share			
Brian			
Lakmani			
Total profit distributed	AUTOSUM		

(b) **Complete the current accounts for the two partners as at 31 December 20X7 in accordancewith the partnership agreement.** **(6 marks)**

	Brian £	Lakmani £		Brian £	Lakmani £
			Balance b/d	-	3200
	AUTOSUM	AUTOSUM		AUTOSUM	AUTOSUM

Section 6

SAMPLE ASSESSMENT – ANSWERS

ASSESSMENT INFORMATION

You have **2 hours and 30 minutes** to complete this sample assessment.

- This assessment contains 6 tasks and you should attempt to complete every task.

- Each task is independent. You will not need to refer to your answers to previous tasks.

- The total number of marks for this assessment is 80.

- Read every task carefully to make sure you understand what is required.

- Task 3 and Task 4 require extended writing as part of your response to these questions. You should make sure you allow adequate time to complete these tasks.

- Where the date is relevant, it is given in the task data.

- Both minus signs and brackets can be used to indicate negative numbers unless task instructions state otherwise.

- You must use a full stop to indicate a decimal point. For example, write 100.57 not 100, 57 or 10057.

- You may use a comma to indicate a number in the thousands, but you don't have to. For example, 10000 and 10, 000 are both acceptable.

SCENARIO

Task 1 is based on a workplace scenario separate to the rest of the assessment

Task 2 to **Task 6** are based on the workplace scenario of BLM & Co.

You are a part-qualified accounting technician working for BLM & Co, a business which manufactures and sells sinks. BLM & Co is owned and run by Brian and Lakmani Moore in partnership.

You cover all aspects of bookkeeping and accounting for the business, along with Jed Malone, who isresponsible in particular for completing the VAT return.

BLM & Co also uses the services of Addo & Co, a firm of accountants. Keira Jackson is the accountant at Addo & Co who carries out tasks for BLM & Co.

TASK 1 (15 MARKS)

Wajid is an accountant who works for Laleham Ltd, a large organisation with many employees.

Tara, a new accountant with Laleham Ltd, has made two statements to Wajid about how she believes the ethical code applies to her.

(a) **Identify whether the following statements are true or false.** (Maximum 2 marks)

Statement	True	False
'I have no duty to act in the public interest provided that I act in the interests of Laleham Ltd and the accountancy profession.'		✓
'The ethical code provides detailed rules on how I should act in every possiblesituation that I might encounter at work.'		✓

(b) **Identify whether or not the ethical code specifically requires Tara to take each of the following actions in order to act in line with the principle of professional behaviour.**

(Maximum 2 marks)

Action	Required	Not required
Comply with all regulations that affect Laleham Ltd.	✓	
Promote the reputation of the profession at every opportunity.		✓

Wajid has noticed that Tara does not conduct her work thoroughly and she often completes it late. He believes that, as a result of Tara's lack of diligence, she is in breach of one of the fundamental principles.

(c) **Identify which fundamental principle Tara has breached.** (Maximum 2 marks)

	✓
Integrity	
Professional competence and due care	✓
Objectivity	

Tara has been told that she is facing disciplinary procedures because she has behaved unethically.

(d) **Identify whether or not each organisation below may bring disciplinary procedures against Tara for her unethical behaviour.** (Maximum 3 marks)

Organisation	May bring disciplinary procedures	May NOT bring disciplinary procedures
AAT	✓	
The National Crime Agency (NCA)		✓
Laleham Ltd (Tara's employer)	✓	

Employment regulations require employers to pay workers at least the National Minimum Wage (NMW).

Laleham Ltd makes high levels of profits. The Chief Executive insists that managers should be paid a veryhigh rate with regular bonuses, but workers should receive only NMW, with no entitlement to bonuses.

(e) **Identify whether the following statements are true or false.** (Maximum 2 marks)

Statement	True	False
The Chief Executive's policy on employee pay raises doubts about the ethical nature of the leadership and culture of Laleham Ltd.	✓	
Because Laleham Ltd complies with the NMW regulations, it is automatically considered to be behaving ethically in relation to its employees.		✓

Ian is an accountant who has just started working for Penton Ltd, reporting to Hettie, who is also an accountant. Ian has discovered a material error in Penton Ltd's last corporation tax return.

(f) **Identify the action Ian must now take.** (Maximum 2 marks)

Action	✓
Resign	
Advise HMRC of the error without disclosing any information to Hettie or Penton Ltd	
Tell Hettie about the error and recommend that Penton Ltd disclose the error to HMRC	✓

Hettie realises that she has inadvertently become involved in Penton Ltd's money laundering operation.

(g) **Complete the following statement.** (Maximum 2 marks)

Hettie may have a defence against a money laundering charge if she makes **an authorised disclosure** to the relevant authority.

Options
a protected disclosure
an authorised disclosure
a prompt disclosure

TASK 2 (12 MARKS)

Today's date is 15 January 20X8.

You are checking an invoice that was issued to a customer yesterday. The invoice is incomplete

From: BLM & Co 200 -210 Farm Road Endsleigh EN61 7DS	To: Emporium Ltd 178 Judd Road Endsleigh EN62 8SP	Invoice date: 14 January 20X8	Invoice number: CJL69840
Purchase Order: 3214	Deliver date:27/12/X7		
Description	**Quantity**	**Per unit** **£**	**£**
Jade 1.5 bowl and drainer	15 units	145.00	2,175.00
		VAT at 20%	0.00
		Total	2,175.00

(a) Calculate the VAT amount for this invoice and the new invoice total. (Maximum 2 marks)

VAT to include on this invoice: £	435
Invoice total including VAT: £	2,610

(b) Identify what the impact on BLM's profit for the year is, if the invoice error is not corrected. (Maximum 1 mark)

	✓
BLM's profit will be higher.	
BLM's profit will be lower.	
BLM's profit will not change.	✓

Jed Malone, your fully qualified colleague, has refused to change the invoice as he doesn't want to upset thecustomer by increasing the invoice amount.

(c) Identify what your next action should be. (Maximum 1 mark)

	✓
Send a Suspicious Activity Report to the National Crime Agency.	
Tell Brian and Lakmani about your concerns.	✓

You discover that BLM & Co has been supplying sinks to Malone Ltd, a company owned and run by the brother of your fully-qualified colleague, Jed Malone. When you look at the relevant invoices, you realise thatJed has been overstating sales and misrecording VAT. As a result, Malone Ltd qualifies for a 15% trade discount on its future purchases from BLM & Co.

(d) **Applying the conceptual framework from the ethical code, complete the sentence below todescribe the situation faced by Jed when recording sales to his brother's company.**

(Maximum 2 marks)

_____GAP 1_____threat to_____GAP 2_____.

Gap 1 Options	✓	Gap 2 Options	✓
A self-review...		objectivity.	✓
A familiarity...	✓	professional competence and due care.	
An intimation...		professional behaviour.	

You conclude that the deliberate misrecording of VAT is unethical behaviour by Jed.

(e) **Identify what your next action should be.** **(Maximum 1 mark)**

	✓
Notify HMRC of the VAT error.	
Tell Brian and Lakmani about your concerns.	✓

On the morning of 16 January, Jed is dismissed for misconduct by BLM & Co and leaves the office. You aretemporarily BLM & Co's only member of the finance team. A VAT officer will be coming to the office for a planned visit on the afternoon of 16 January. You are not prepared for this visit and do not believe you can answer any questions from the VAT officer effectively. Brian and Lakmani insist that you must be present and deal with the VAT officer without assistance.

You feel intimidated by Brian and Lakmani's insistence that you must be present to deal with the VAT officerunassisted.

(f) **Identify what your next action should be.** **(Maximum 1 mark)**

	✓
Resign from BLM & Co.	
Seek external advice from AAT.	✓
Agree to deal with the VAT officer in line with your employers' instructions.	

Because of Jed's misconduct, Brian and Lakmani have asked you to examine his recording of sales ledgertransactions for the three months ended 31 December 20X7. You identify the following information:

Sales ledger control account balance at 1 October 20X7: £492,409

From 1 October to 31 December:

- Receipts from credit customers: £934,076

- Sales to credit customers, including VAT: £970,370

- Returns from credit customers, including VAT: £21,177

- Irrecoverable debts written off, including VAT: £4,330.

Amounts owed at 31 December 20X7, as confirmed by credit customers: £487,354.

(g) **Drag each of the four options below to the appropriate column to reconstruct the sales ledgercontrol account for the three months ended 31 December 20X7.**

(Maximum 2 marks)

Sales ledger control account

	£		£
Balance b/d	492,409	Cash book	934,076
Sales day book	970,370	Sales returns day book	21,177
		Journal (irrecoverable debt)	4,330
		Balance c/d	487,354

Options:

Cash book	934,076
Sales day book	970,370
Sales returns day book	21,177
Journal (irrecoverable debt)	4,330

(h) **Calculate the missing figure in the sales ledger control account.**   **(Maximum 1 mark)**

£15,842

(i) **Identify which of the following the missing figure could represent.**   **(Maximum 1 mark)**

	✓
Discounts allowed.	✓
Direct debit from customer returned unpaid by the bank.	
Cash sales.	

TASK 3 (13 MARKS)

Today's date is 31 January 20X8.

From the cost accounting records, you can see that on 1 January 20X8, BLM & Co had 8,000 kg of raw material inventory. The cost recorded was £18,000. In January 20X8, the following movements took place:

6 Jan: 1,600 kg purchased for £3,440

11 Jan: 3,200 kg purchased for £7,360

13 Jan: 9,200 kg issued to production

The partners want to know how the remaining inventory of 3,600 kg would be valued using the FIFO methodof cost accounting.

(a)   Using the FIFO method, value the inventory held on 31 January.   (Maximum 2 marks)

£8,220

(b)   Identify which of the following is the correct journal for recording the year-end inventory.
(Maximum 1 mark)

	✓
DEBIT Purchases, CREDIT Closing inventory (current asset)	
DEBIT Closing inventory (current asset), CREDIT Purchases	
DEBIT Closing inventory (current asset), CREDIT Closing inventory (cost of sales)	✓
DEBIT Closing inventory (cost of sales), CREDIT Closing inventory (current asset)	

BLM & Co manufactures jade sinks in batches of 20. In the last production run in 20X7, the following costswere incurred for the batch:

	£
Direct materials	1,020
Direct labour	960
Prime cost	**1,980**
Variable production overheads	240
Fixed production overheads	280
Fixed non-production overheads	100
Total costs	2,600

At 31 December 20X7, three jade sinks were held in inventory.BLM & Co usually values inventory at full absorption cost.

(c) **(i)** **Explain how inventory of unsold sinks is valued differently depending on whether marginal orfull absorption cost is used. You must show your workings.**

(Maximum 4 marks)

When inventory is valued at marginal cost, only the variable costs of producing each item are included in thevaluation. (1) This includes the prime cost and the variable production overheads. (1)
For the Jade sink, the marginal cost per unit is £111 (1) ((1980+240)/20) so the three sinks held in inventorywould be valued together at £333. (1)
When inventory is valued at full absorption cost, a share of fixed production overheads incurred by thebusiness is included in the valuation (1), so the valuation is higher under absorption costing. (1)
For the Jade sink, the absorption cost per unit is £125 (1) ((1980+240+280)/20) so the three sinks held ininventory would be valued together at £375. (1)
Note that, irrespective of method, the non-production overheads are not included in the inventory valuation.(1)
(Maximum 2 marks for marginal; maximum 2 marks for absorption)

(ii) **Explain the effect of using the two different methods mentioned in (i) on the partnership'sreported profit. You must show your workings.** **(Maximum 2 marks)**

In the year ended 31 December 20X7, if the partners had valued the Jade sinks at marginal cost rather thanfull absorption cost, reported profit would have been lower (1) by £42 (375-333) (1), because the share of fixed production overheads was expensed in 20X7, the year of production, rather than being absorbed into inventory, carried forward and expensed in the year of sale. (1)

As at 31 December 20X7, BLM & Co's closing inventory valuation was £36,800. The partners expect to make sales of £3,190,000 in 20X8, and they expect the inventory valuation to rise by 10% by the year end. The gross margin is expected to be 45%, after deducting direct materials and direct labour.

(d) **Calculate how much BLM & Co expect to spend on direct materials and labour in 20X8. You must show your workings.** **(Maximum 4 marks)**

£	£	£
Sales		3,190,000
Opening Inventory	36,800	
Materials/labour (balancing figure)	1,758,180 (2 marks)	
Closing Inventory (36,800*1.1)	(40,480) (1 mark)	
COS (55%)		(1,754,500) (1 mark)*
GP (45%)		1,435,500

* this mark can be for COS or GP calc

TASK 4 (15 MARKS)

Today's date is 28 February 20X8.

Brian has asked you to prepare some financial statements urgently. These include a statement of cash flowsand a cash budget. He needs to send these to the bank by the end of the week as part of a loan application. Brian tells you that obtaining the loan is very important for the survival of the business. The jobs of everyonein the business depend on this. You have not yet studied statements of cash flows or cash budgets.

(a) **(i)** **Identify TWO threats to your ethical principles as a result of Brian's request**

(Maximum 2 marks)

> I am facing familiarity, intimidation and self-interest threats (1) because the partners of BLM & Co are tryingto appeal to my loyalty to colleagues and fear of losing my job. (1)

(ii) **State what response you should give to Brian in order to remain ethical.**

(Maximum 1 mark)

> I would tell Brian that I can only complete the tasks they have requested if I have additional training/qualifiedsupport/supervision to do so (which will take time) (1) **OR** I would tell Brian that I cannot undertake the task competently so it should be given to someone else. (1)

(iii) **State ONE reason for your response to Brian.** **(Maximum 1 mark)**

> I do not have the experience, expertise (knowledge and skills), or time to complete the tasks properly. It would be a breach of the principles of professional competence and due care, and integrity, to attempt to doso immediately. (1)

Your role at BLM & Co includes:

* supporting sustainability throughout the business

* measuring sustainability in the business.

(b) **State why you, as an accountant, have a professional duty to uphold sustainability in your work.** **(Maximum 1 mark)**

> Because ensuring sustainability is in the public interest and accountants have a responsibility to work in thepublic interest. (1)

You receive the following email from Lakmani Moore:

To: Sam Jones <Sam.Jones@BLMCo.co.uk>
From: Lakmani Moore <Lakmani.Moore@BLMCO.co.uk>
Date: 28/2/X8
Subject: BLM & CO: change in structure

Good morning Sam,

Brian and I are considering operating the business as a limited company.

I would like you to tell me more about the implications of a partnership becoming a limited company. Please include three sections in your response to me as follows:

1   A brief description of a limited company

2   A summary of our position as owners if the business becomes a limited company

3   Explanation of one key advantage and one key disadvantage of operating as a limited company

Regards,

Lakmani

(c)   Write an email to Lakmani, addressing all points that have been raised.

(Maximum 10 marks)

1   A brief description of a limited company
1 mark for reference to the following indicative content:
Separate legal entity / distinct from owners
Must be registered at Companies House
Company's accountants and finances are separate from personal finances of its owners
(Maximum 3 marks)
2   A summary of our position as owners if the business becomes a limited company
1 mark for reference to the following indicative content:
Owned by shareholders
Managed by directors
Must be at least one shareholder
Both Brian and Lakmani can continue to be owners if both have shares
Could be other owners
After-tax profits re-invested in the company for shareholders
Dividends / salaries
(Maximum 3 marks)

3	Explanation of one key advantage and one key disadvantage of operating as a limited company

1 mark for reference to the following indicative content:

Advantages:

Limited liability for owners

Company as separate legal entity remains fully liable for its debts

Company can continue to exist even if shareholders die

Shareholders can share in the profits of a company, even if they don't work for it

(Maximum 2 marks)

Disadvantages:

Heavily regulated

Accounting regulations / statutory requirements of Companies Act 2006 / accounting standards

Greater administrative burden than for a partnership / greater administrative cost

Must file accounts each year before a certain date / subject to audit

Details widely available for third parties to see

(Maximum 2 marks)

TASK 5 (12 MARKS)

BLM & Co has two profit centres, Retail and Manufacturing, and one support cost centre, Administration. Administration supports the two profit centres with 70% of its time spent with Retail and 30% of its time withManufacturing.

The budgeted overheads for the quarter ended 31 March 20X8 are shown below. You have been asked to help with the allocation and apportionment of the overheads.

Budgeted overheads	£	£
Depreciation		153,725
Rent and rates		130,000
Salaries		354,750
Retail	98,900	
Manufacturing	137,600	
Administration	118,250	
Total		638,475

The following information is also available:

Department	Carrying amount of machinery £	Power usage kWh	Floor space Sq M
Retail	19,500	22,000	750
Manufacturing	195,000	198,000	1,250
Administration	0	0	1,000
Total	214,500	220,000	3,000

(a) Complete the following overhead apportionment table. Show your answers to the nearest whole pound. Use minus signs where appropriate. **(Maximum 6 marks)**

Overhead apportionment table

(Note: in the computerised version the totals would calculate automatically)

Budgeted overheads	Basis of apportionment	Retail	Manufacturing	Administration	Total
Depreciation	Carrying amount of machinery	1,3975	139,750	0	153,725
Rent and rates	Floor Space	32,500	54,167	43,333	130,000
Salaries	Allocated	98,900	137,600	118,250	354,750
		145,375	331,517	161,583	638,475
Reapportion administration		113,108	48,475	-161,583	
Total		258,483	379,992		638,475

Options:
Administration
Carrying amount of machinery
Depreciation
Floor space
Machinery at cost
Power usage

You have been asked to flex the original budget based on actual activity.

(b) **Complete the following table. Show your answers to the nearest whole pound.Adverse variances must be denoted with a minus sign or brackets.** (Maximum 6 marks)

	Original budget £ 5,000 units	Flexed budget £	Actual results £ 6,000 units	Variance £
Sales revenue	1,240,000	1,488,000	1,500,000	12,000
Variable costs	597,000	716,400	705,200	11,200
Fixed overheads	638,475	638,475	638,875	-400
Operating profit	4,525		155,925	

TASK 6 (13 MARKS)

Note: This task is human marked. Students will be required to make text and numeric entries in both thepartnership appropriation statement and the current account.

You are preparing the final accounts for BLM & Co for the year ended 31 December 20X7. The statement ofprofit or loss for BLM & Co shows a profit for the year ended 31 December 20X7 of £247,982.

For the year ended 31 December 20X7, in accordance with the partnership agreement:

- Lakmani is entitled to a salary of £25,000 per year

- interest on capital has been calculated as £4,350 for Brian and £2,850 for Lakmani

- Brian has taken drawings of £91,200 over the year, and Lakmani has taken drawings of £84,400

- interest on drawings has been calculated at £300 for Brian and £180 for Lakmani for the year

- the residual profit after adjustments is shared between Brian and Lakmani in the ratio 3:2.

(a)   Complete the partnership appropriation account in accordance with the partnership agreement for the year ended 31 December 20X7. Show your answers as positive and to the nearest whole pound. There does not need to be an entry in every space.

(Maximum 7 marks)

Partnership appropriation statement for year ended 31 December 20X7

	Total	Brian	Lakmani	Marks
Profit for the year	247,982			**1 mark** for correct figure in 'Total' cell
Add				
Interest on drawings	480	300	180	**1 mark** for whole row, including label – can be in any row, but must be "Add"
Total	480			
Less appropriation of profits				
Salary	25,000		25,000	**1 mark** for whole row, including label – can be in any row, but must be "Less appropriation of profits"
Interest on capital	7,200	4,350	2,850	**1 mark** for whole row, including label – can be in any row, but must be "Less appropriation of profits"
Total	32,200			
Profit available for distribution	216,262			**1 mark** for Profit for the year + total of "add" – total of "appropriation of profits" (OFR allowed)
Profit share				
Brian	129,757			**1 mark** for correct figure (OFR allowed)
Lakmani	86,505			**1 mark** for correct figure (OFR allowed)
Total profit distributed	216,262			

(b) **Complete the current accounts for the two partners as at 31 December 20X7 in accordancewith the partnership agreement.** **(Maximum 6 marks)**

	Brian £	Lakmani £		Brian £	Lakmani £
Interest on drawings	300	180 (1)	Balance b/d	1,200	3,200
Drawings	91,200	84,400 (1)	Salary	0	25,000 (1)
			Interest on capital	4,350	2,850 (1)
			Profit for the year	129,757	86,505 (1)
Bal c/d	43,807	32,975 (1)			
	135,307	117,555		135,307	117,555

Marking guidance:

- 1 x mark for each correct row
  - All elements must be correct, including label
  - Entry must be on correct side
  - OFR allowed for Profit for the year figures
  - OFR allowed for Bal c/d figures